P9-CBR-810

The Creative Word

FORTRESS PRESS BOOKS
BY WALTER BRUEGGEMANN

*The Land: Place as Gift, Promise, and Challenge
in the Biblical Faith* (1977)

The Prophetic Imagination (1978)

*The Creative Word: Canon as a Model
for Biblical Education* (1982)

David's Truth in Israel's Imagination and Memory (1985)

Hopeful Imagination: Prophetic Voices in Exile (1986)

Israel's Praise: Doxology against Idolatry and Ideology (1988)

Finally Comes the Poet: Daring Speech for Proclamation (1989)

*Interpretation and Obedience:
From Faithful Reading to Faithful Living* (1991)

*Old Testament Theology:
Essays on Structure, Theme, and Text* (1992)

*Texts under Negotiation:
The Bible and Postmodern Imagination* (1993)

*A Social Reading of the Old Testament:
Prophetic Approaches to Israel's Communal Life* (1994)

The Psalms and the Life of Faith (1995)

*The Threat of Life:
Sermons on Pain, Power, and Weakness* (1996)

The Creative Word

Canon as a Model for Biblical Education

WALTER BRUEGGEMANN

FORTRESS PRESS   PHILADELPHIA

Biblical quotations from the Revised Standard Version of the Bible, copyright 1946, 1952, © 1971, 1973 by the Division of Christian Education of the National Council of the Churches of Christ in the U.S.A. are used by permission.

COPYRIGHT © 1982 BY FORTRESS PRESS

All rights reserved. No part of this publication may be reproduced, stored in a retrieval system, or transmitted in any form or by any means, electronic, mechanical, photocopying, recording, or otherwise, without the prior permission of the copyright owner.

Library of Congress Cataloging in Publication Data

Brueggemann, Walter.
  The creative word.
  Includes bibliographical references and index.
  1. Bible O.T.—Canon. 2. Christian education.
I. Title.
BS1135.B74   221.1'2   81-71387
ISBN 0-8006-1626-X (pbk.)   AACR2

Printed in the United States of America   1-1626

12   13   14   15   16

Contents

Preface

This book seeks to make a statement at the interface between two disciplines: my own discipline of Old Testament study and the discipline of education. Such a book is possible only when two risks are taken, and I have taken both. First, it is necessary to be somewhat synthetic and sweeping about one's own discipline. I have tried to do that in judicious ways and intend not to be reductionist. Second, one must presuppose some things about the second discipline at the interface. I have made these presuppositions, which I hope are responsible, even if not fully informed.

The chapters of this book were prepared primarily for the Caldwell Lectures given at Louisville Presbyterian Theological Seminary in March 1981. Regarding that lectureship, I especially thank President Ellis Nelson and my host Craig Dykstra for their kind hospitality. Along the way, portions of this material were also given as the J. Clyde Wheeler lectures on ministry at Phillips University School of Religion and at Ewert College in Toronto. In those places as well, I was kindly hosted and graciously received, even if not uniformly agreed with.

This book has been long in the brooding stages. Initially the topic formed for me in response to an invitation from Larry Kalp of the United Church Christ. Near the end of the process my colleague, Ruby Schroeder, read the manuscript and provided helpful suggestions. Moreover, I have especially to thank several of my colleagues, my students for bearing with some exploration, and a host of friends who operate in the educational "network" of the church. Matty Ebersbach helped prepare the manuscript. And supremely, the two Marys in my life have been involved all along the way. My secretary, Mary Waters, presides over my special form of written communication. Mary, my wife, attends critically and supportively to hints that even fall short of that mode of writing. To finish the manuscript is to be grateful to them.

WALTER BRUEGGEMANN
Eden Theological Seminary

1
Canon and the Educational Repertoire

Every community that wants to last beyond a single generation must concern itself with education. Education has to do with the maintenance of a community through the generations. This maintenance must assure enough continuity of vision, value, and perception so that the community sustains its self-identity. At the same time, such maintenance must assure enough freedom and novelty so that the community can survive in and be pertinent to new circumstances.[1] Thus, education must attend both to processes of continuity and discontinuity in order to avoid fossilizing into irrelevance on the one hand, and relativizing into disappearance on the other hand.

The Old Testament mirrors a community that intended to last over the generations. Therefore the Old Testament had to be concerned with education. To be sure, this concern is not very often explicit in the text. But it is clearly a persistent and pervasive concern nonetheless, as the community struggled with continuity and discontinuity. And as the Old Testament itself seldom addressed education frontally, so Old Testament scholarship has seldom taken this concern as a useful entry into the text. Indeed, the secondary literature that considers these issues directly is surprisingly limited, surely to our disadvantage.[2]

There are two reasons why I have decided to take up these issues. First, I suspect we are at a time when there may be an important interface between Scripture study and education in the church.

Church education has been intensely interested in the social sciences and has indeed learned much from them. Nothing said here is meant to detract from the positive attention to learning theory, learning process, developmental psychology, and cultural anthropology which have greatly influenced the awareness of the church. In the next decade, critical sociology is likely also to have an important say. But in the midst of attention to the social sciences, I suggest that the biblical, theological disciplines have not been a full partner. The interface, therefore, has not been a very balanced one. Our concern here is to ask if Old Testament study can be a more effective partner in the dialogue about education, both constructively and critically. One can detect a move away from an uncritical embrace of the social sciences not only in education, but also in "pastoral care" and what we have come to call "organizational development."

Second, after some decades of confusion, it appears that current approaches to church education are relatively clearly defined. Most of these approaches can be linked to one or more prominent leaders in the field. The enterprise is thus divided into camps revolving around certain agendas and methods, or we may say, certain ways of putting the question. It is convenient for study to have things stabilized in this way, even to the making of an inventory. And indeed, Jack L. Seymour has helpfully offered such a summary list.[3] It includes:

1. Religious instruction approach, in continuity with the Sunday school movement (James Michael Lee).
2. Socialization and enculturalization (John Westerhoff).
3. Spiritual development, informed by developmental psychology (James Fowler).
4. Liberation, which is concerned with the mission of the community (Malcolm Warford).
5. Systems education, which attends to congregational formation (Robert Worley).
6. Interpretation praxis (Thomas Groome).

This may be a fair summary of where we are, though someone will no doubt be annoyed at being omitted from the list. But that still leaves the unanswered question of where we go next. I am proposing that an interface with Scripture study might contribute to the next steps we need to take as colleagues in a common ministry. That is the "external" reason for addressing the issue. And by "external" I mean simply a motivation that lies outside my own discipline of Old Testament study.

The "internal" motivation for addressing this topic is that the current shifts in Old Testament study itself suggest possibilities for a fresh interface with education. Without completely abandoning the enterprise, Old Testament study now seeks to move beyond historical-critical analysis into other perspectives and methods. It is clear that these moves are required and permitted by new interfaces with various social sciences. The enterprise which perhaps holds most promise for our subject is what is loosely called *canon criticism*. As we shall see, that general term is used to refer to a variety of things. Canon criticism rests in the awareness that *how* the biblical material reaches its present form (canonical *process*) and the *present form* that it has reached (canonical *shape*) are important theological matters that tell us about the intent of the biblical community. In other words, the Bible-shaping process cannot be viewed as a neutral or incidental process which can be studied with critical indifference. The shaping process is itself a confessional act. By studying that process and its end result, we can learn much about the community's self-understanding and its intent for the coming generations. Thus the broad link I suggest is that *canon is a clue to education, both as substance and as a process.* One reason Scripture study of a historical-critical variety has been unable to address education as a biblical theme is because canon was bracketed out as a secondary, irrelevant, or mechanical process that had nothing to do with educational claims or intentions. Still, if canon is neither an unexamined given nor an unintended accident, but an intentional transmitting process, then clearly it concerns education. The discussion I propose is simply this: Attention to the process and shape of canon may tell us something about education in ancient Israel. In addition, it may provide clues for our own educational task, which I suggest is aiding communities and their members in the ongoing task of canon construction and canon criticism.

Our beginning, therefore, is with *canon criticism*, even though there is no agreement about the meaning of the phrase.

1. Canon criticism clearly has roots in tradition criticism, especially as articulated by Gerhard von Rad.[4] As is well known, von Rad identified certain texts, specifically Deut. 6:20–24, 26:5–9, and Josh. 24:1–13, as the summary of Israel's faith.[5] These summaries he called "creeds" or "credos," but he might well have called them the preliminary canon.[6] That is, these summaries became the normative expression of community faith. To be sure, von Rad located these normative expressions in the liturgy. But it is clear, especially in Deut. 6:20–24[7] and in the credos generally, that liturgic or otherwise, these served an educational function. Von Rad has helped us see that the community, in its liturgy and elsewhere, did attend to the educational, nurturing, socializing agenda. And von Rad's understanding of these credos shows that they were both *continuous* in repeating the same data and *discontinuous* in receiving new data and extending the statement toward new contemporaneity.[8] So already the argument is that if the community of faith is serious about education, it must attend to the canonical, credal process.[9]

2. Brevard Childs has most fully addressed the concerns of canon.[10] As I understand him, his agenda is to find a way into the Bible that moves beyond the historical-critical tendency to relativize. That is, a method must be found to respect the judgment of the community that these texts are normative and enduring, true and reliable, and not to be explained away by criticism. Childs' way of argument is to address the canonical shape of each book of the Old Testament, to argue that the way the book now stands, regardless of the process, is in itself a theological statement of a normative kind.

Childs's program and achievement are staggering. But it is not clear how it will help us in our enterprise for two reasons.[11] First, Childs is not interested in the *process* of canon, but only in its final *shape*. While such a focus is surely legitimate, it does not advance our investigation very far because it brackets out the dynamic to which we must attend. And indeed, Childs must bracket it out to make his point about the claim of the text beyond criticism. Second, Childs approaches biblical books one at a time. That is problematic because one never gets a sense of the whole of the Bible or of the whole of the Old Testament. As I hope to show, that may be our most helpful clue.

3. A much more usable approach is that of James Sanders who, in contrast to Childs, attends to the canonical *process*, that is, to the dynamic by which these materials function to become and to continue as normative. In his book on the subject,[12] Sanders pays attention to the tripartite order of the Old Testament and sees that there are different degrees and kinds of authority, that each has a distinct role to play, and that this threefold character admits an important dynamic in the development of a sure authority.

In a more recent article,[13] Sanders has shown that canon, in order to maintain its authority, must be both "stable" and "flexible"; it must partake both of continuity and discontinuity. In ancient Israel the tripartite canon (law, prophets, writings) permitted and articulated this requirement. It is important that Israel formed and valued all three parts of the canon, kept them in relation to each other, was relatively clear about the function and place of each, and never tried to make one of them substitute for another. Sanders's principle of stability and flexibility, while not simply to be overlaid upon the three parts of the canon, does tell us what to look for. It permits us to notice that over a period of time the emergence of the later, younger parts of the canon (prophets and then writings) continues the principle of flexibility. The older part of the canon, Torah, becomes increasingly removed not only in time, but also in its mode of shaping the issues.

4. Canon criticism as a way of discerning a process is closely related to redaction criticism. Here we should recognize especially the work of Ronald Clements,[14] Joseph Blenkinsopp,[15] and more recently, Gerald Sheppard.[16] Redaction criticism is, among other things, a study of the way the Bible uses the Bible, reinterprets the Bible, claims an old text and restates it in a new form for a new day.

The relationship between *old text* and *new expression* is dialectical and delicate. It clearly is a traditioning process that both honors and takes the old text seriously (thus stability); at the same time, however, it gives freedom to a fresh articulation (so flexibility).[17] Specifically, Sheppard[18] has argued that there has been a sapiential traditioning process in which Old Testament texts have been recast according to a new epistemological frame. He says that this process has not just added a new piece of canon, but has decisively impinged upon the old material as well. Thus the dynamic of canon requires that it not just remain open-ended. It is a dialectical process in which new claims are either recognized in or assigned to the old materials. The wisdom process thus represents a remarkable response to a radically changed situation. But the new response is made completely on the grounds of the old tradition.

Sheppard has rightly seen that this *process* (so Sanders)[19] which has *reshaped* the literature (so Childs) constitutes a major hermeneutical move. It is not a neutral literary process or simply a translation to get from one period to another; it is, instead, engaging the text in subtle ways as the live Word of God which can give vitality to the community. This hermeneutical enterprise permits the text to continue to have vitality, authority, and relevance for new generations in new circumstances.[20] This suggests, then, that the hermeneutical enterprise is something church educators can no longer regard as outside their responsibility.

Such an approach to Old Testament study clearly holds enormous promise for us. It places in a new context much of the old historical-critical learnings to which we are witnesses and heirs. As educators, we should pay attention to the canonical process in Israel. For if we can understand how Israel dealt with these difficult matters of continuity and discontinuity, of stability and flexibility, we may arrive at a new sense of authority in education. We may understand afresh how the Bible is the live Word of God. We may even come to see education in the church and outside the church not as a professional, rational enterprise, but as a calling that is urgent both for survival of the community and for the faithfulness of the community.

This, then, marks our starting point: *the process of canon is a main clue to education,* a process which partakes of stability and flexibility, continuity and discontinuity. By attending to this confessional act, we may avoid the hazards of rigid *fossilization* which hold to a frozen, unresponsive canon, and to a deep *relativizing* which gives up everything for a moment of relevance. The canonical process is not done by outsiders or by calculation or by professional educators. It is a confessional, theological act done only by those for whom everything is at stake. It follows that the *educational process,* faithfully carried out, can be performed only by those who submit to the *canonical process.* Everything is at stake for them in the educational process because that process is intimately linked to the canonical process, where everything is likewise at stake. There is not a learner in the church, young or old, who is not in fact engaged in the process of canon. My concern is to address the intentional educational task of the church. But I would also insist that every formal and informal act in preaching, in liturgy, and in pastoral care (even counseling) is a canonical enterprise of probing the normative, of casting off old pieces of canon that are no longer vital, and of embracing new aspects of canon which address us inescapably. Canon has to do with life. And in the end there can be no noncanonical life or ministry which can have any sense, meaning, joy, or certainly, staying power.

We may begin our consideration with Jer. 18:18, a verse often cited as a way of entry into the canon. The verse poses serious difficulties. It is attached to the complaint of vv. 19–23, but it does not seem to be an integral part of the complaint.[21] Rather, it is a quote set in the mouth of Jeremiah's opponents. Its function appears to be an attack upon the authority of the prophet.

The verse is nicely framed in an *inclusio*:

at the beginning: Come, let us make plots against Jeremiah. . . .

at the end: Come, let us smite him with the tongue, and
                              let us not heed any of his words.

It is not clear who Jeremiah's opponents are, or what the plot is.[22] But what is important for us is that inside the summons to conspiracy is a summary of Israelite authoritative knowledge:

Surely *(kî)* the Torah shall not perish from the priest,
    nor counsel from the wise,
    nor word from the prophet.

Perhaps the conspirators convinced themselves that they could proceed against Jeremiah because the knowledge structures and the authority structures were sure and reliable. Therefore, this particularly troublesome man was dispensable. It may give us some pause about education in a community of faith that the modes of knowledge and the authoritative offices are here bracketed by a summons to eliminate them. The structure of the passage suggests how precarious instruction is in Israel, perhaps because of how subversive it is perceived when faithfully done.

But what interests us is the middle part of the verse, which identifies three sources of knowledge and three authoritative offices. If the verse stems from the seventh century, as seems plausible, we suggest that these three modes are not late developments which can be arranged chronologically. This old assumption can no longer be sustained, especially about wisdom. Rather, the threefold pattern here points to parallel and persistent modes of knowledge and education which must have been operative from of old in Israel. If we therefore want to understand education in its fullness, we must take all three into account:

the Torah of the priest,
the counsel of the wise,
the word of the prophet.

The three agents of instruction are identified as priest, wise, and prophet. The three shapes of knowledge are said to be Torah, counsel, and word. Each of these, I shall argue, has a special *substance* and a distinct *mode* in the life of Israel. And a faithful community must attend to all three, not selecting one to the neglect of the others, or subordinating one to make it conform to the others.

As a grid for what follows, two general comments may be made about the shape of the Old Testament canon as hinted at in Jer. 18:18.

First, the canon is divided into three parts, three layers of literature which came to be regarded as authoritative in different times with different degrees of intensity. I shall argue that each of these three parts of the canon (summarized in Jer. 18:18) has a different *function* in Israel, proceeds with a different *epistemology*, and makes a different *claim* in Israel.[23]

1. The Torah, the first five books of the Old Testament which are conventionally called Pentateuch, claims the most basic authority. The specific question concerning Mosaic *authorship* is a modern question posed from wrong premises. There is no doubt, however, that the material claims Mosaic *authority*, which is something other than Mosaic authorship. This literature, of course, is fundamental for all that comes after it in the Bible. And it follows that this material is foundational for education.

2. The prophets come next after the Torah both in rank of importance and in the time of its stabilization as a body of literature. Thus the first two parts of the canon are grouped together as normative in those references to the "law and the prophets," or better, the "Torah and the prophets" (Matt. 5:17, 7:12, 11:13, 22:40; Luke 16:16, 29, 31, 24:27; John 1:45). This grouping of normative texts includes four books—Joshua, Judges, Samuel, and Kings—termed "former prophets"—four corresponding scrolls—Isaiah, Jeremiah, Ezekiel— and the twelve (minor prophets)—termed the "latter prophets." Thus the two groups together, former and latter, form a nice symmetry. It is important that the books we conventionally call "history" are regarded as books of the prophets. That is, they do not chronicle the affairs of persons and nations, but they trace the impingement of God's Word and purpose in, with, and under historical experience.

3. The third part of the canon, latest and least important, is the Writings *(kethubim)*. This is a miscellaneous collection of everything else in the Old Testament. We can tell from the earliest translation of this material that it is not regarded as rigorously authoritative, since it is handled with relative carelessness. Freedom is exercised by translators that would have been unthinkable for the Torah of Moses. Thus even the method of translation suggests we are here dealing with a literature of some slippage and freedom. And it is clear that only later

on was the formal issue of the normative character of these materials settled. Of these various books, the most important surely are the Psalms, Job, and Proverbs. Probably it is especially the kind of material in the Book of Proverbs which is attested to in Jer. 18:18 as the "counsel of the wise." The shape (with various different orders of arrangement) and the looseness of translation suggest that at the time this material was being collected and edited, the category of canon had been relaxed or had lost its importance. That also is an important educational observation.

We thus begin with an awareness of this threefold structure, the relative authority of each collection, and the dynamics of the relation of each to the others. Perhaps Matt. 23:34 alludes to these structures in its reference to prophets, wise men, and scribes, especially if scribes are understood as the knowledgeable interpreters of the Torah of Moses.

Second, for each part of the canon, we will consider two distinct but related questions. On the one hand we will ask the *substantive* question: What does this literature suggest about *what Israel knows?* This question is related to Childs' concern for the *shape of the canon,* for the substance of the literature as it stands. On the other hand we will ask *how Israel knows what it knows.* That is, what is the process by which Israel comes to know? This question is related to Sanders' concern for the *process of the canon.* It is likely that *what Israel knows* and *how Israel knows* are closely linked. *Shape and process, how and what, substance and method* are bound together. Educators are not permitted to focus exclusively either on the substance of knowledge or on the processes of knowing, but must attend to the correspondence between the two. We shall suggest as we go along that there is a peculiar match in these three instances to the *how and what* of Israel's education.

Finally, I suggest that educators in the community of faith—by personal inclination and conviction, by church tradition, by social setting, and for various other reasons—are drawn toward one part of the canon or another to the relative neglect of the others. And we are drawn to one part of the canon or another both for the substance of what is taught and learned and for the process of how it is taught and learned.

1. Conservative persons or church traditions will be inclined to focus on the how and what of the Torah, on the how of the most authoritative instruction and on the what of Israel's most stable articulation of faith. Such education addresses what is "always and everywhere believed among us." It is taught with certitude and urgency.

2. Social critics, radicals, and revolutionaries will most likely be attracted to the prophetic canon. Those who incline toward social change will attend to the explosive, intruding word of the prophetic. That will be important both for the mode of epistemology, being committed to the coming of "new truth," and to the substance of criticism and "unmasking" that marks the prophets.

3. Humanistic psychologists, those who follow the more or less rational modes of John Dewey and those who care for human potential and actualization, may well be drawn to the third part of the canon, to the "counsel of the wise," which appeals to "persuasiveness" and "obviousness." This part of the canon, especially with reference to the buoyancy of the Proverbs and the anguish of Job, are, on the face of it, more attuned to experimental learning and authority.

It is my hunch that in the more liberal spheres of church education, which are the ones I know best, a relatively comfortable, uncritical, peace has been worked out between adherents of the second and third parts of the canon. These educators, however, need to take seriously also the first part of the canon, the Torah, without yielding those gains. Conversely, in more conservative settings, deep adherence to the modes and claims of the Torah may now be set in a context of the danger of the second or the risk of the third part of the canon. I propose that church education, both in its modes and its substance, has gone awry precisely because of the failure to hold these three parts of the canon, these three normative modes of disclosure, in balance and in tension. Imbalance in this regard leads to an imbalance of method and derivatively, to an imbalance in the kinds of knowledge and the shapes of questions that are considered valid and pertinent.

I hope that a consideration of the educational claims of the tripartite canon may serve us in two ways. First, it should give us fresh insight into our own inclinations and the likelihood of our tilt toward some particular, unwitting but not disinterested posture. Second, it should open possibilities for recovering the balance, for attending especially to the how and what of the canon, which is not our most likely inclination. In approaching the issue in this way, I suggest that these tensions, imbalances, and possibilities in church education are not new matters. They may be presented in fresh form. But the emergence of an overall canon in this threefold shape suggests that our community has always struggled with the issue. There have always been those who preferred the Torah of *certitude* from the scribe or the *freshness* of word from the prophet or the *hunch* of counsel from the wise. Always in Israel, these folks had to listen to each other and be reminded that not any one of them could author the entire tradition. It is the invitation of canon to educators that we should have a varied repertoire of both mode and substance, and that we should have a keen sense of which season requires which part of the canon.

As an overview of the following argument, let me identify three accents I shall try to make for the three parts of the canon, that is, for the three tasks of education. Regarding the Torah, I shall argue that it is a statement of community *ethos*, a definitional statement of the character of the community which is a given and is not negotiable among the new generation. In this first part of the canon, it is clear that the community precedes the individual person, that the community begins by stating its parameters and the perceptual field in which the new person must live and grow. In the Prophets, we deal with the *pathos* of God and of Israel, with the sense of fracture and abrasion between what is in hand and what is promised. This part of the canon expresses the conviction that such abrasion is not overcome by power or force, but by hurt. Therefore this part of the canon reflects on indignation and also on the anguish which belongs to this community and its perception. Third, in the Writings, we cannot in fact generalize for the whole. In the Proverbs at least, that is, in the "counsel of the wise," we may speak of the *logos*,[24] of the conviction that there is sense and order and meaning to life. That logos is hidden and revealed. Education is the cat and mouse game of discovering and finding it hidden (Prov. 25:2-3).[25]

These are the themes that I will develop. The shape of the argument and the mode of presentation require that we speak about them one at a time. But in the end, I will want to insist upon the unity of the canon. For good education, like Israel's faith, must be a tense holding together of *ethos, pathos,* and *logos.* While we must avoid being reductionist about these three, the one thing we may provisionally say about them together comes as a hint in Jer. 18:18. Such education, such ministry rightly done is *radically subversive.* It evokes resistance and hostility. That should not surprise us. That indeed is the condition of church education. Any educator who hopes to avoid that abrasion by focusing on one aspect alone cannot claim to be facing the whole canon in all its richness.

2

The Disclosure
of Binding

Our beginning must be with the Torah, where Israel always begins. Here I take the term to refer to the five books of Moses, though in other contexts, of course, the term Torah has other referents. Israel in all generations believes, with the enemies of Jeremiah (18:18), that the Torah of the priest will not perish. So we begin with the first division of Israel's canon and with Israel's most authoritative literature.

The five books of Moses as they now stand, however, were not given to us in their fixed form. While we may attend to the *shape* of the canon, we must go behind it to consider the *process* of canon. That is, how did these books come to us? For our purposes the obvious place for educators to begin is with the question asked of the parent by the child, or of the priest/teacher by the learner. In the Old Testament, that question has six variant forms, but all of them raise the same point:

"And when your children say to you, 'What do you mean by this service?' you shall say . . ." (Ex. 12:26);

"And you shall tell your son on that day . . ." (Ex. 13:8);

"And when in time to come your son asks you, 'What does this mean?' you shall say to him . . ." (Ex. 13:14);

"When your son asks you in time to come, 'What is the meaning of the testimonies and the statutes and the ordinances which the Lord our God has commanded you?' Then you shall say to your son . . ." (Deut. 6:20–21);

". . . that this may be a sign among you, when your children ask in time to come, 'What do those stones mean to you?' Then you shall tell them . . ." (Josh. 4:6).

"When your children ask their fathers in time to come, 'What do these stones mean?' then you shall let your children know . . ." (Josh. 4:21).[1]

These six variant forms are placed in quite different situations in Israel. Together, they make a primary point: The beginnings of the Bible manifest concern for the educational process.[2] I should like to argue that this is the taproot of the completed form of the Torah. I think it can be sustained that in this early, simple-but-quite-stylized form, Israel is already engaged in the canonical process. These exchanges are the starting point for the literary, *canonical* process, as well as for the *educational* process. This concerns us, since I am convinced that the educational enterprise can never be far from the canonical process.

The six questions and answers clearly are not objective historical reporting. Nor are they a dogmatic conclusion that is being insisted upon. They are not an exercise in literature to satisfy an aesthetic function. In part, they are aimed at worship, but clearly worship as pedagogy, the engagement of the young in the normative claims of the community. These six exchanges show the binding of the generations, the urging toward a view of reality held by the older generation as definitional for the new generation.[3] That it is urgent and normative and must be binding, that is, canonical, is evident in the closely related instruction:

> And these words which I command you this day shall be upon your heart; and you shall teach them diligently to your children, and shall talk of them when you sit in your house, and when you walk by the way, and when you lie down and when you rise (Deut. 6:6–7).

Such is the canonical process in the Torah of Israel.[4]

NARRATIVE AS ISRAEL'S PRIMAL MODE OF KNOWING

Let us begin by considering *the mode of knowledge*, the way in which Israel here knows what it knows. Of course Israel was not

modern and scientific in reflecting upon the learning process. But
such communities also were not stupid. By imitation and experience,
modes of learning were practiced which did the job.

The exchange in the form of question and answer is *quite
unauthoritarian* but utterly *authoritative*.

1. The occasion of the teaching is open and easily dialogical. It
occurs in a context which has been set up to evoke interest, curiosity,
and wonderment on the part of the children. Ritual is context-cre-
ating in the case of the passover (Exodus 12–13), in the giving of the
commandments (Deut. 6:20–24), and in the crossing of the waters
(Joshua 4). The ritual serves to evoke a teachable moment, not contained or coercive but expected in these ceremonies of remembrance
and reflection. On these occasions, Israel capitalized on the yearning
to belong and to understand, to penetrate these marvelous mysteries
of the adult world which seem to be so precious and satisfying.
Authority is evident in the capacity to keep a secret and then, at the
right time, to share a secret.[5] Education in Israel begins in the yearning of the children to belong to the secret. Teaching is perhaps the
shrewd management of that secret, having an acute sense of when
and in what ways it is appropriate to conceal and when to reveal.

2. The adult response to the yearning of the children is the articulation of the creed, or if not creed, at least classical, highly stylized
testimonies to faith. The answer given is a set recital, not an answer
made up on the spot. The base line of identity for the community is
known. Adults are capable of articulating it. These stable, known
answers announce what is normative for both generations. It is not
asked if the hearing children will find the answer convincing or binding, or if they will find it too heavy or complicated or parochial or
embarrassing. And it is not asked if the adult who speaks it has misgivings or reservations. The elemental educational moment is un-
complicated, unencumbered, and unembarrassed. Undoubtedly such
responses can be asserted in such unequivocal ways because the
answering adults themselves have a passion and nerve for what is
being said. The answering adults live in a world that has not yet faced
questions of self-doubt. Torah, "the Torah of the priest," could not

have been formed by people with misgivings. Nor could it have been used by people who had misgivings. Thus Torah, the first element of Israel's canon, educational process, and faith lives and works in a "pre-doubt world."

Now of course there were misgivings in Israel. We should not be romantic and line things up chronologically as though first there was "dreaming innocence" and then came the doubts. The doubts must surely have been there from the beginning. We know that is true because Moses' leadership is in conflict and dispute from the beginning (Exod. 2:14; Num. 11:4–15, 12:1, 14:2, 16:1–2). But I would argue that for the canonical and educational enterprise, the misgivings by definition occur *within* the context of Torah, that is, on the basis of these sure memories. They do not get a hearing behind, before, beyond, or underneath the Torah. The Torah functions as the context for doubt and misgiving. Because of that, the Torah has a voice in shaping the form and character even of the misgivings.

Now that is important. It says something about the educational context in which we work. The implication is not that the Israelites were undiscerning primitives, but that certain educational enterprises must take place in certain contexts. As we shall see later with wisdom, some of the education was precisely concerned with "the practice of misgivings." But not Torah. Torah is a protected, privileged enterprise in which all those tendencies are bracketed out. This fundamental instruction is the practice not of *suspicion* but of *naiveté*. And the naiveté must be practiced by both learner and teacher. Belief-full naiveté then becomes the context for subsequent practice of suspicion. The church may nurture its members in such naiveté.

3. Contrary to our humanistic education and to our catechetical tradition, in the Torah of Israel it is a child who asks and a teacher (priest, parent) who answers. In contrast to humanistic education, this mode of education does not assume that the child must locate a normative answer in his or her own experience, as though immediate experience yielded credo insights on the spot. Children are not expected to do this in Israel because normative articulations of faith are not individual, private conjurings. Moreover, in contrast to the

catechetical tradition in which children memorize the right answer and parrot it back, the role of the child here is openness and wonderment. Nothing about the exchange is heavy or dictated. This should stimulate considerable thought, since so much church education has bounced back and forth between heavy catechetical instruction imposed on the learner, and privatized faith in which persons are pressed to be authors of their own faith. In the Torah we have a mode of teaching, I submit, which means to avoid both of these tendencies. A third way appears to be possible precisely because the teacher has no failure of nerve, and this is a privileged enterprise with the doubts screened out. Children are not asked to screen out everything permanently. I shall argue that the other aspects of canon provide an important dialectical corrective to this screening out. But for the moment, both parties suspect their suspicion and engage in childlike affirmation.

This mode of canonical instruction believes that the normative articulations of faith lie outside the individual human psyche, exist before us, wait for us, and are given to us as a gift.[6] Children need not invent world-forming secrets; but they are invited to share in a secret already trusted and relied upon.

The answer is given by the one who claims the answer as his or her own. The answer is given by an adult who has enough passion to bear the answer as truth. Israel is a community that "has its story straight."[7] The story can be told as a base line. It is given by adult to child with confidence, nerve, passion, delight. So I suggest as an epistemological structure: Knowledge in the Torah is a gift given with *firmness*, because it is undoubted—with *graciousness*, because there is eagerness to share—with *authority*, because the speaker both owns and is possessed by the story. This clearly contrasts with so much of what passes as church education today. We know better how to evoke the child's wonder than we do how to give a normative answer which functions as premise and not as conclusion.

But think what is being entrusted from one generation to another! It is nothing less than and nothing other than Torah. The word *Torah* is so comprehensive and fuzzy that we struggle with it. At least it does not mean "law."[8] It is the Torah of the priest, given by one who sorts out "what's what,"[9] one who is charged to tell the truth. It is given by the one who can spot the dangers and who can locate the edges of safe and viable conduct and imagination in the community. It is done by those who have a due sense of how to survive and prosper in the presence of this troublesome, threatening holiness. That is what children learn in this exchange. They learn the truth—our truth. Soon enough children know there may be somebody else's truth.[10] But Torah is not so complicated. Our truth is the truth that holds and binds us for now.

There is something in that for us, who want to be so tolerant and so understated and so fair about the truth. So much of our education has been the management of alternative "truth claims." Educators become those who manage the process of considering alternatives. As we shall see, that is indeed the work of other parts of the canon. But not here. Not in Torah. When your child asks you in time to come, you shall not say, "Well, it might mean that we came out of Egypt, or it might mean we are faithful slaves in Egypt, or it might mean we are fascinated with the rituals of Canaan. And you choose among these." No! In this moment there are no alternatives. This is the truth![11] This is what it means, and we are not prepared to doubt it. That same teacher at other times of the day—in the still of the night or in the late afternoon—may have entertained alternatives and practiced other parts of the canon. But in this context, in this stylized exchange, both parties face the truth of this community.

Perhaps it helps if we risk rendering Torah as the Greek does—as nomos.[12] But we must not take nomos in a narrow, legalistic sense as Lutherans are inclined to do. Let us rather take it as the sociologists suggest, as an articulation of world coherence, as a shaping of reliable order, as a barrier against the chaos that waits so close (cf. Jer. 5:22). The answer of these six questions sets out an orderly, reliable life-world in which children can find coherence and assurance, in which they can understand and celebrate who they are vis-à-vis the strange darkness of chaotic waters and in the face of the ominous threats of Egypt, Canaan, and Babylon. Education in the Torah is participation for the next generation in a safe life-world. It is offering that life-world and creating that life-world. It is ushering the child into that life-world.

A community of nurture and socialization does not simply socialize into religious practices. Rather, it engages in the construction of a world, the formation of a system of values and symbols, of oughts and mays, of requirements and permissions, of power configurations.[13] The five books of Moses thus build again and again a presumptive world about which there is a genuine consensus. And we may take note that the consensus is possible because there is no attempt to modernize, to make contemporary, to interpret, or to link it to any present issue. In itself, the "root consensus" makes few concrete demands. The reason, I suggest, is that these educators recognized that the most basic convictions of the community would stand on their own, without defense, support, argumentation, or application. These convictions could be asserted in their boldness and left to stand. They would do their own work. They would hold under scrutiny. The single legitimating factor beyond their intrinsic claim was the passion of the adult community for response. The ground needed was a parental generation that did not doubt.

This matter of life-world, presumptive world, ethos, and consensus is indeed urgent. Life must be a gift before it can be a task. It must be there waiting for us and not constructed by us, though eventually we may participate in the ongoing world construction. The Torah is Israel's yearning that its children should not grow up in chaos, in alienation, in narcissistic subjectivity. Robert Merton has offered a characterization of a Torah-less world, though he does not use that language[14]. The word for it is "a-nomos," without order, normless, anomie. A normless world is not a world for self-actualizing individuals. Rather, it is a jungle of competing, savage interests. We are at the edge of that in our culture, for the consensus has collapsed. And I dare say that much of the immobility of the church is because of a theological normlessness, Torahlessness, is when everyone does what he or she pleases, except that soon our desire is skewed, emptied, failed, boring. The Torah is a line drawn against the darkness and disorder, against the Canaanites and Egyptians, but finally against the chaos and death that waits.

We talk here as though this matter concerns a gift the older generation can give to the young. That is how our texts present the matter, and our experience agrees with that. But we may enter a reservation that is surely important. Torah is not just for children. Anomie is not a danger only for the young; it may surface in what is now conventionally called the "crisis of mid-life" or anywhere else. All persons face the threat of the darkness. All persons, no matter how smart or how rich or how mature, grow weary of dispute and questioning and risk. All persons need those times of "homecoming" when they can return to the sureties which do not need to be defended or doubted. And that is what Torah is. It is a homecoming, like putting feet under mother's table where the old food and the reliable topics and the safe presuppositions are all at work again. So the questions we have focused on are for the young. But education in this community must provide opportunities for all persons to return to those privileged times of discourse which cut underneath the dread and the suspicion back to the naiveté, like childhood. Therefore:

> When all Israel comes to appear before the Lord your God at the place which he will choose, you shall read this law [Torah] before all Israel in their hearing. Assemble the people, men, women, and little ones, and the sojourner within your towns, that they may hear and learn to fear the Lord your God, and be careful to do all the words of this law [Torah], and that their children, who have not known it, may hear and learn to fear the Lord your God, as long as you live in the land which you are going over the Jordan to possess (Deut. 31:11–13, cf. 20:10–15).

There is a tilt from the old to the young. But Torah is finally intergenerational.

We may note one other aspect of this fundamental educational exchange.[15] There is important slippage between the question and the response. The seeker asks the question, "What do these stones mean?" which demands an explanation. But the response refuses an explanation. There is a shift in mode, and this is important to education. The *mode of articulation* must match *the substance to be articulated.* In the very shift of mode, the community of adults announces to the child what kinds of epistemology are possible in this community. Many things are not known in this community, and some ways of knowing are precluded. Many things are bracketed out, not known, not asked about. The Torah does not answer every question. It picks the ground quite selectively. The response of the adult is authoritative. It does not let the child determine the ground. But it is also honest to the child. It concedes ignorance. More than that, it honors mystery. It assures the child that there is much that we do not know and cannot know. So the question perhaps cannot be answered in the form in which it is asked. What does the question of the child mean?

The adult answers characteristically, "Let me tell you a story." It is our story, but still only a story. That is all that has been given to us. In that way the child learns both about the *deep conviction* of the adult and about the *precarious foundation* of our faith. The child learns that this parent commonly refuses to be sucked into other knowledge games, refuses to know too much, and refuses to give in to people who want to know too much for the wrong reasons (for example, Mark 11:27–33, 12:13–17).

The primal mode of education in the church, derived from the Torah, is *story.* There is a crucial match between the mode of story and the substance to be told. Trouble surfaces in the community of faith whenever we move from the idiom of story. As soon as we make this move, we create an incongruity between our convictions and the ways we speak our convictions. When we are saddled with this incongruity, we spend our energies on alien questions:

Do you believe the Bible is inerrent? . . . let me tell you a story . . .

Do you believe Jesus was raised physically from the dead? . . . let me tell you a story . . .

Do you believe we should ordain homosexuals? . . . let me tell you a story.

Admittedly, the response of "story" will not satisfy all. I do not pretend that it is an adequate response for every issue, but it is our

primal and most characteristic mode of knowledge. It is the foundation from which come all other knowledge claims we have. That
reminds us, too, about how provisional so much must be. What Israel
knows is that if the story is not believed, nothing added to it will
make any difference. That is why the commandments of Sinai are
always grounded in the surprise of liberation from Egypt. If one does
not believe in the surprise of liberation, then the endless multiplica-
tion of commandments from Sinai is silly, for more commandments
without the foundation of the Exodus story will never create a community of well-being. So education in Israel is based on "let me tell
you a story"—not just any story, but this one which we have found
reliable.

Recently, much has been made of theology and storytelling.[16] Simply because it has been emphasized lately does not make it less important. Story as a distinctive way of epistemology is especially appropriate to Torah and includes these points:

1. Story is *concrete*. It is about particular persons in particular times
and places. It does not flinch from the scandal of specificity. There is
no pretense of universal truths. Similarly, good church education
must stay with such concreteness and must avoid every universaliz-
ing temptation.[17]

2. Story is *open-ended* in its telling. While there is insistence in
ancient Israel that these are the proper stories without alternative,
there is no comparable insistence that they be told in a certain way.
The storyteller, once he or she has been claimed by these stories, has
enormous freedom for the telling—freedom not only to give different
nuance and accent, but freedom to turn the wordage in one direction
or another. We have enough data in terms of doublets and evidence of
redaction to know that there was not only a *consensus* about which
stories, but a matching *flexibility* in their telling. The reason for this
is that the community was not concerned to communicate static
meanings or flat memories to Israel's new generation. Rather, it was
concerned about creating a context, evoking a perception, forming a
frame of reference which went beyond and did not depend on any
particular version or nuance of any particular narrative.

Thus storytelling of a Torah kind requires as much flexibility as it does fidelity. But notice what a different notion of freedom. This is not freedom which permits a new story or requires self-projecting innovativeness. Rather, this is freedom which operates in a context, knowing the boundaries of form and plot and characters. Inventiveness means that the characters in this plot are given full play for themselves.

3. Story in Israel was intended for the *practice of imagination*. That is, there is no straight-line communication of data from speaker to listener. There is an open field of speech between the parties that admits to many alternative postures. This means that the listener has nearly as much freedom as the speaker in deciding what is happening. The listener is expected to work as resiliently as the teller. The communication between the two parties is a bonding around images, metaphors, and symbols that are never flattened to coercive instruction. Israel has enormous confidence in its narrative speech, sure that the images and metaphors will work their own way, will reach the listener at the point of his or her experience, and will function with a claiming authority. Such communication is shared practice of the secret which evokes imagination.[18] It includes the listener in the secret, thus forcing the awareness of an insider. And it serves to draw a line on the other side of the listener, distancing the listener from all the outsiders who do not know the secret.[19] That is, once the secret is known, it cannot be not known. The telling of the secret evokes imaginative work in the listener. Thus the practice of imagination moves, on the one hand, with liberation. The listener has freedom to hear and decide, and is expected to decide. On the other hand, however, the story moves with authority to claim people for the inside. The authority that moves through it is not only the authority of the teller, but also the authority of the story. Israel's imagination is liberated and liberating. That does not mean unlimited and undisciplined, as though anything goes. The imagination of Israel is circumscribed by the scope of the stories about which there is consensus. Israel has a covenant with its tongue, that the evoking of imagination does not move outside this consensus. We shall see that in the other parts of

Israel's canon, there is a breaking beyond this consensus. For the Torah, however, it is enough to accept the consensus and to move around in it fully. It is the consensus on which stories are based that defines the arena for free imagination.

4. Stories in Israel are characteristically *experiential*. That is, they tell what happened, what we have seen and heard, what happened to us. They are told by participants, not by objective third parties who tell someone else's stories. The adults do not ask children to believe stories by which they themselves are not claimed. Now, having said that, it is perfectly clear that the stories live across the generations. Not all of Israel's storytellers lived at the time of Moses or Samson or Elijah. So when we say experiential, we must not understand that notion in personalized or privatized or immediate terms. Rather, we must talk about the *public experience* of Israel which encompasses each new generation.

The matter of public experience across the generations is an urgent one for Israel's education. Obviously this is no easy notion in a culture beset by narcissistic individualism and subjectivity. A curiosity of our time is that such a narcissistic environment should nurture appeal to timeless universal myths. But there is a nice match between such *individualism*, which reduces to psychological categories, and *timelessness*, which escapes the dangers of history. Israel's storytelling, however, denies both of these temptations, so that one is not free to have a *private faith* and not free to embrace the *common myths of the dominant culture.*

The Torah is for the nurture of public experience. Such a notion is not simply making the best of a bad situation, but is an urgent insistence upon the communal character of human life and the strange processes of transmission and inheritance in the historical community. It is simply not true, so Israel would claim, that personal immediate experience is adequate for life. The community, some community, countercommunity, or anticommunity, shapes perception and governs personal experience. Not only is private experience not adequate for life, it is a deception to speak of private experience; for all human experience is deeply social. As there is no "presuppositionless exegesis" of the text, so there is no "presuppositionless experience" of life.[20]

Therefore the poetic, liturgic capacity to move back and forth between the generations is not a rhetorical trick, but helps define the life of Israel (cf. Deut. 5:3; 29:15). Israel's narrative awareness is in deep conflict with a powerful ideology of our time. It critiques every presentation of "I only believe what I see," not because it is dangerous to believe this (which it is), but because it is wrong. Social forces shape the "I" as well as the seeing and the believing. Those social forces are not only spiritual and religious, but economic and political as well. None of us is going to get outside the influence of those forces. Israel's insistence on public experience is based on that awareness. Israel knew very well that the alternative to this *public* experience is not *private* experience, but rather the *alternative public experience* of Egypt or Canaan or Babylon. Thus Israel's public memory, which is transmitted in these narratives, serves at the first level as a guard against anomie, of having to reinvent one's own world. At a deeper level, Israel's public memory is a counterexperience, a subversive alternative to an imperial consensus. Every time Israel tells one of its stories, it means an assault on and refutation of another one. This point is important and has been lost on much church education. We have been gently benign, as though our stories were simply casual alternatives to some others also worthy of consideration. Or it is as though our stories were only a bit "more true," but not enough to press about. Not so for Israel. Israel understood that in its Torah, done by its most authoritative teachers, everything was at stake. For the narrative means to dismantle alternative worlds as well as to construct new ones for the listening community.

5. Story in Israel is the *bottom line*. It is told and left, and not hedged about by other evidences. It is not like a preacher who adds two paragraphs after the manuscript, as if to buttress and reinforce it. Israel has confidence in its stories, in and of themselves. Israel understands them not as instruments of something else, but as castings of reality.[21]

Perhaps that is Israel's epistemological message to its own. We trust the stories because there is a deep match between the mode of the story and our public experience. We rely upon memory, which becomes experience in the process of imaginative retelling. It must be left at that. Any who want to get behind the story are looking for a ground more basic than Torah, and such a ground is not available to Israel.

Thus the mode requires educators to settle for a modest enterprise. Israel does not propose to offer a story which is true for everyone all the time. Israel makes no claims or assertions of "eternal truths." Israel's Torah is not a list to be printed on a pencil to pass about indiscriminately in the street, as would a beggar. Israel's narrative is too precious and too dangerous to be passed around so casually. It must be guarded and cared for, treasured and celebrated, kept intact with form preserved.

That is the case because Israel's narrative is a partisan, polemical narrative. It is concerned to build a countercommunity—counter to the oppression of Egypt, counter to the seduction of Canaan, counter to every cultural alternative and every imperial pretense. There is nothing in this narrative that will appeal to outsiders who belong to another consensus, or who share a different ethos and participate in another epistemology. To such persons, Israel's narratives are silly, narrow, scandalous, and obscurantist. The narrative form of the Torah intends to nurture insiders who are willing to risk a specific universe of discourse and cast their lot there. It is a significant and telling fact that the more we want to present a culture religion that accommodates the epistemology of the dominant regime, the more we are pressed to flee the Torah to other parts of the canon. The question was always alive in Israel: Shall we risk these stories? Shall we take our stand on them? If we do, we must do so with the awareness that not only the substance, but our modes of knowing are suspect and troublesome in the world. The question continues to be problematic for educators: Can we risk these stories? The answer is known only when we decide if we want to subvert the imperial consciousness and offer a genuine alternative to the dominant forms of power, value, and knowledge.

THE SUBVERSIVE CONSENSUS OF TORAH

Our consideration of the *mode and process* of Torah now needs to be matched by attention to the *substance of Torah*. What in fact is the Torah about? What does Israel want her children to know? What must every person, young and old, be offered upon homecoming? What is this *subversive consensus* about?

In all six questions the response to the child's quest is either about Exodus/Sinai or, in the case of Joshua 4, the taking of the land. As Gottwald has suggested, in the imagination of Israel we cannot very well separate the Joshua events from the Moses events no matter what the historical facts may have been.[22] The two are now coalesced in the memory of Israel. The ethos of Israel sponsored by the Torah, the perceptual consensus, is constructed around the Moses/Joshua events of liberation. These events are now presented to us as one overriding paradigm.

1. These events are about the *intervention of a new God* whose name was not known before. No matter what interesting history-of-religion data may be summoned, this is Israel's version of reality: the coming of a new lord on behalf of a nameless rabble. Such an incredible narrative is a claim against all conventional religions, ancient and modern. Characteristically, all conventional religion wants to derive and extrapolate, to stress the continuity, to explain everything in terms of antecedents. That is because conventional religion, in its reasonableness, does not believe there is a newness that can come against the system. Everything is at issue in this different perception. There either is a new God who intrudes, even though God's name is not known, or there is not. On that issue hang the crucial claims of biblical faith concerning *creation ex nihilo*, resurrection from the dead, and justification by grace through faith.[23] Either the work of God depends on antecedents which are other than God, or it does not.

The Torah is simple and unambiguous on the point; it is about newness, an underived, unextrapolated discontinuity. So Israel begins its story with the young in a decisive break with every monotheism and every polytheism.[24] Israel's story is against every reasonable explanation, every congenial interface with administered human culture. It is not an appeal to a modern theological theory (Barth!), but is characterized by an abruptness that must in quite unreflective form jolt both hearer and listener. Moses simply does not know the name of this God and is resistant to God's claim (Exodus 3—4).

The narrative of Israel is an announcement of a radically new resolve in heaven that from the world of the gods there emerges this one who is responsive to the groans of the uncredentialed (Exod. 2:23–25). No explanation is given that would satisfy the other gods or that would convince any of the rulers on earth. No speculation is offered which would preoccupy the philosophers or entice the scientists. This is simply a *disclosure,* a surprising announcement of something as true as unexpected, without accompanying commentary. Because of that unexplicated responsiveness from among the gods, there is a genuine newness on earth. Israel, a liberated, cared-for community, comes out of nothing because it lives by answered groans. So Israel's first response to the children—surely without thoughtful preparation—is of a newness wrought in heaven and then become visible on earth. Say the teachers of Israel to the questioning young: "We are that newness!" (cf. Exod. 19:5–6; 1 Pet. 2:9–10). The narrative thrust of Israel's primal educational material is to make available to the learner a new identity. (We can bracket out, as Israel bracketed out, all scientific questions of the relation of Exodus to the pre-Mosaic religion of the patriarchs. This is a difficult question, but not one that delayed these teachers in Israel. Obviously Israel's subsequent traditions proposed various answers to the question,[25] but that is subsequent reasoned reflection). In the first instance, we have abrupt good news. The response of Torah to the question of the child is *gospel!*[26]

Too much cannot be made of this fact: the primary data of Israel's education claims the character of revelation. It is *disclosure.* It is admission to an awareness that has intrinsic authority. Education consists first of all in admitting others to the arena of disclosure to permit new generations to be reidentified by this revelation.[27]

2. The substance of the first response to the children is a story of miracle and wonderment—a disruption, an inversion, an exposure of all conventional human relations. It is, as Buber has seen, an event with "abiding astonishment."[28] The ethos[29] to which the children are invited is one that assures we shall never cease to be astonished, or never be so satiated or numbed or co-opted that we forget the abruptness in heaven and on earth that has caused us to be. We shall never become so domesticated that our lives are not jolted and our cages rattled by the discontinuity. So the new category of miracle becomes a paradigm for self-understanding, valued in every cultural setting and every historical crisis.[30] The narrative consensus assures an abiding restlessness with every present arrangement. Education is to nurture others into this history of restlessness. Now we can see why this substance must have the mode of narrative. How else shall we speak of an urgent matter which defies all the reason and logic of the empire?

3. This "core tradition"[31] is about a *shift in power* among the gods and in the arena of economics and politics. The notion of a shift in power is not a late reflective discernment. It is at the edge of the story; it is what hits us first. The response to the children cannot be narrated in any way which does not focus upon this shift:

". . . he slew the Egyptians but spared our houses" (Exod. 12:27).

". . . with a strong hand the Lord has brought you out of Egypt" (Exod. 13:9).

"By the strength of hand the Lord brought us out of Egypt, from the house of bondage. For when Pharaoh stubbornly refused to let us go, the Lord slew all the first-born in the land of Egypt . . . for by a strong hand the Lord brought us out of Egypt" (Exod. 13:14–16).

Any educator who will engage this material must face Karl Marx's central insight about religion, that is, that every religious conviction and assertion has a counterpart in the arena of earthly power.[32] So education in the Torah is about power. We dare not be insensitive any longer, therefore, to the totalitarian political implications of much educational psychology. Every educational psychology that confines itself to inner, subjective, personal matters is a tacit support of public totalitarianism. The issues of public power are not late addenda, but are the stuff of Israel's ethos. The agenda of the Torah (which "will not perish from the priest") is the transformation and redistribution of power in human affairs. The narrative must be left in its raw unacceptable subversiveness. It will not be reduced to safe religion or personal introspection. There is no child so young that the miracle and gift of power,[33] and the threat of power, is not a primary agenda. The reality and ambiguity of power is fundamental to humanness. The only education which does not know that is education which likes and means to preserve present power arrangements. Education in the Egyptian empire surely tried to bracket out all the power questions. But Israel addresses that issue as its beginning point. The disclosure (revelation) of this narrative is that power has been reassigned.

4. So the Torah is a *celebration of power*, new power for "the groaner." But, then, it also is inevitably a *criticism of power* wrongly assigned and claimed. That is subversive. In the imagination of Israel, the Torah means to delegitimate other power and to dismantle all such systemic claims of power which are incongruent with the dream. Torah begins with the dethronement of Pharaoh. Subsequently, the story moves to an awareness that every power—ours included—is provisional and subject to deep and dangerous criticism. Torah is a dismantling criticism and, at the same time, a proposal for an alternative way.[34] Both the *criticism* and the *alternative proposal* come packaged only as impressionistic narrative.

I have spent a disproportionate amount of time on the Exodus narrative because we have been led there by the pedagogical exchange of child question and adult response. When the child and the adult engaged in reflection, that was their subject. It is clear, however, that the Torah is not encompassed in the single event of the Exodus or in its derivative event, the entry into the land. More briefly we may consider the mode of *narrative*, the intent of *ethos*, and the claim of *disclosure* as it concerns the whole of the Torah.

1. It is now increasingly urged that we must seek to see the Torah

(five books) as a whole, as together making a theological claim. On the one hand, James Sanders[35] has paid special attention to the fact that the narrative of the Torah ends with the death of Moses, short of the land. Moses is permitted to see the land (Deut. 32:48–52; 34:1–8), but is not permitted to enter it.[36] To be sure, the book of Joshua comes next, but not in the Torah. The Torah as normative ethos is landless.[37] Therefore it leaves Israel with hope, with not having arrived, but with sure trust that there will be a fulfillment.

Complementarily to Sanders, David Clines has urged that *promise* is the central theological claim of the Torah.[38] That is an exceedingly important discernment for education in the church. The certitude of promise, the reliability of the Promise-Maker and Promise-Keeper is the datum of the Torah. To nurture the young or not-so-young in this faith is to evoke in them the sense that promise is definitional. The Torah is the announcement of the promise, the slow painful keeping of the promise, and a reflection of what to do (obedience) while waiting. The promise as a rallying point for the community functions: (a) to deny the notion of a closed, fixed fate—against this, it argues that we are bearers of a destiny that is still working its way; (b) to prevent the despair and numbness that come with hopelessness—the Torah is a barrier against the erosion of giving up; and (c) to preclude a settling in on the present no matter how good it is. The promise of the yet-to-be-given makes us restless with, free from, and critical of any present circumstance. Thus the seeds of revolution are found in this promise.

2. When the Torah is seen in its wholeness, the main disclosure is of a God who makes promises and will keep them. Under that general and somewhat reductionist rubric, we may comment briefly on several elements in the Torah which cluster around the Exodus account beginning, of course, with the "prehistory" of Genesis 1—11. This prehistory has already been terribly overstudied, and we need not restate all of what has been said. The following observations, however, may be important.

Out of these early narratives, we may teach a binding between Creator and creature. Binding as an instructional motif is against most of the ideologies of our time. The binding is shrewdly summarized in Gen. 2:15–17 in three elements:

binding as *vocation*: "to till it and to keep it"

binding as *gift*: "you may freely eat of every tree of the garden"

binding as *prohibition*: "but of the tree of the knowledge of good and evil, you shall not eat . . ."

It is unfortunate that the popular version stresses the prohibition, for in these three verses the three motifs are held together. These three together constitute a good summary of the ethos that Israel entrusts to its young. In the middle of the blessing comes the "tree of command."[39] The tree of command is not law, not punishment, not burden, but simply the way life is discerned in Israel. God "commanded." The verb is "command." At the very beginning, already at creation, Israel understands life to be under command.[40] Consequently, I should argue that the very structure of creation is picked up in the catechetical tradition of Deut. 6:20–24:

> And the Lord commanded us to do all these statutes, to fear the Lord our God, for our good always, that he might preserve us alive, as at this day.

The motifs of Deut. 6:20–24 are strikingly parallel to those of Gen. 2:15–17: "good/preserve/alive." The teaching of the children moves from Genesis 2 to Deuteronomy 6. In such a way there is remarkable coherence in the themes of the Torah.

A second pause in this great and familiar narrative is the flood story. This story moves in a strange way from 6:5–8 to 8:20–22, or in the P element, from 6:9–33 to 9:1–17. As is well known, the story begins in the grief (not anger) of God and in the assessment of human imagination as evil. That is the starting point. What is not so often noticed is that the flood story ends in the same way, with the human imagination still evil (8:21). What has changed is the resolve of God, which moves from grief to new fidelity. The flood story does not speak about human transformation or even about punishment, but about a change in the heart of God. The shocking good news is the change caused in God. Bernhard Anderson has seen that 8:1 is the center of the flood story.[42] Everything is changed, only because God remembers. The surprising thing about this God, who has both a past and a future, is that he acts differently in the present and toward the future because of the faithful minority in the past (cf. Gen. 19:29; 30:22; Exod. 2:24). Again, as we move from these narratives to Deuteronomy, even the land is given, in part, because of God's memory. I single out this text because the ethos of Israel has a disclosure about God that is at odds with the usual religious notions of our culture. It is a scandal that God should be *moved to change* rather than standing firm while humanity changes. God is not immune or inaccessible, but is moved by the reality of human life.[42]

Third and finally in this material, there is a telling phrase at the end of the Tower of Babel story (Gen. 11:1–9)—v. 7 has it that the people may not "understand one another's speech." That is the conventional rendering. But the text has *lo' shema'*, that is, they did not listen to each other, would not hear. Such a precise rendering changes things considerably. The norm of Israel knows that we are *ear people*, made to listen and to answer (cf. Deut. 6:4). But something happens where there is no faithful speech. I take it that a Torah-centered education is the nurture of persons to listen to the commandments of God, to the promises of God, and to the voice of the neighbor. If we may envision a counterculture which is genuinely listening, it will be a dangerous threat and alternative to the primal culture that is fully against the ear. Thus, in a third way, the motif of Genesis 1—11 is picked up in Deuteronomy. Humanity unable to hear is now summoned afresh to listen.[43]

In all these ways—under *commandment* (Gen. 2:16), being *remembered* (8:1), and *hearing* (11:7)—the ethos of Israel is already made clear. It is to these themes that the teaching of Deuteronomy returns, and it is at these dimensions of reality that instruction in Israel is aimed.

3. The ancestral narrative is the story of promise (Genesis 12—50). It is given by the storytellers of Israel. But the promise for which the story is a vehicle is from the speech of God. It is without justification

given to those "as good as dead" (Heb. 11:12). In each generation it is given to one that is precarious:

a. It is given to the unworthy, even when they do not trust in it.

b. It is a present power of life, even if the substance is only in prospect (cf. Hebrews 11). That is, the speech of promise as such, our memory tells us, enables persons to continue in life and in faith.

c. Most important, the promise is not fulfilled, not even at the end of Genesis: "And all these, though well attested by their faith, did not receive what was promised, since God had foreseen something better for us, that apart from us they should not be made perfect" (Heb. 11:39).

The strange notion of promise is fundamental to this ethos.[44] Both aspects of promise are crucial: it is utterly *trusted* and it is quite *unfulfilled*. In the great commentary on the promise in Hebrews 11, the conclusion drawn in v. 40 is that the significance of the ancestral lives depends on the faithfulness of the children. In this ethos, Israel knows that everything in this entire sequence *depends on the next generation.*

4. In the Torah of Israel, of course, the bulk of the material is what we may call "law." Exodus, Leviticus, and Numbers contain a great deal of such material. For our time, it is important that the Bible is not interested in uncritical, undialectical freedom. To be sure, it also is not interested in uncritical, undialectical obedience. A more fundamental term is *righteousness,* even though that term has been overlaid with moralism and pietism. Both freedom and obedience belong to the "new righteousness of God" (cf. Matt. 5:17–20; Rom. 10:1–4).

To the extent that this material is instruction to the young, we have a lot to learn here about education. First, Israel wants to be clear with its young that there is command. One not only has to decide, but one has to accept the norms of this holy authority. In the Torah, this is not debatable. It is given for all to accept. Second, it is commonly affirmed that there is only one commandment to which everything else is simply exegesis. That dominating commandment is: "There will be no other gods before me." This is a claim of exclusive loyalty.

This assertion cuts both ways: it is a radical criticism of every easy,
tolerant polytheism and henotheism; and it asserts that there is a God
who will have our devotion.[45] The commandment refutes *autonomy*
as much as it refutes *tolerance* among the gods. It is possible that this
first commandment is not in fact a commandment at all, but a victory
cry:

There will be no other gods . . .

(because I have come and defeated the other gods).[46]

This suggests that education in the church is to be focused on God.
This issue must be faced again and again, because the key issue is
always image making and idol worship. Israel knows that the God-
question cannot be bracketed out, and we may not assume it is settled. For as soon as the God-question is assumed settled, we grow
careless. Ethics become autonomous, and theology loses its critical
edge in the church.

The exclusive claim of Yahweh over all of life is handled in two
ways in the Torah: First, *the holiness of God* is a proper concern of
education. The awesome, overwhelming, terror-evoking reality of
God is not instrumental. It is an end in itself. Thus the proper goal of
human existence is indeed "to glorify God and enjoy God forever."
The holiness of God redefines our life and our purposes. It assures
us, on the one hand, against the assumption that the mystery of life is
given over to us. It assures us, on the other hand, against the despair-
ing assumption that there is no mystery of life. The decalogue
teaches about God's freedom, the awesomeness of time (Exod.
20:8–11), and the awesomeness of language (Exod. 20:7) as the modes
of life which must be guarded. These are protests against the exhaust-
ing profanation of life.

Israel believed that a concern for the holiness of God is a proper
and urgent matter. Israel's Torah did not rush out to comment on
every issue of the day. Much of that will be handled from other voices
who are knowing and responsible. But what is peculiarly entrusted to
us is the issue of God's holiness. Sometimes a focus on the holiness of
God means running the risk of appearing to be irrelevant and "uninvolved."

Second, the exclusive claim of God is linked to the *value of the brother and the sister.* God's claim is the critical principle which permits my turning away from my own good and my own interest to that of the neighbor. This twofold structure of the holiness of God *for himself* and *for us* is articulated:

in the structure of the decalogue, in the "two tablets";

in the argument of Leviticus, "Be holy, for I am holy";

in the twofold summary of commandments by Jesus (Mark 12:28–34).

The battle is to keep these together. In the church tradition I know best, we would prefer to rush past the matter of *God's holiness* to the question of *human justice.* In other contexts, the contrary danger may be evident. Without the holiness of God, the justice of neighbor becomes a crusade rather than a vocation. So we must hold these together. I submit that education in this textuality requires, of all things, that we consider again the majestic juxtaposition of themes as they are presented, even in Leviticus.

Finally, concerning the Torah, we must comment upon Deuteronomy. There is no doubt that Deuteronomy is a pivotal piece at the end of the Torah. It is also intentionally a teaching literature and is likely the theological center of the Old Testament. Deuteronomy does not accommodate itself easily to other elements of the Torah as such and perhaps is a misfit there. But I suggest a playful connection between the *earth* of Genesis 1 and the *land* in Deuteronomy. Both are *'ares,* the same word. The earth, which is so universal and ill-defined in the creation narrative, has now become the specific and identifiable *land* of promise in Deuteronomy. While the land—the coming into property and prosperity, well-being, security and substance—is the real payoff of Torah religion, it also presents a deep problem for the faith of Israel. Because of its problematic character, the Torah pauses a long time at the Jordan in the Book of Deuteronomy before crossing.[47] The land has been the agenda since Genesis 1, when the first creatures were given a "good

earth." But after all that has transpired, Israel still has the question:
"Can one be obedient in the land?" Israel knows that you cannot take
the deep mysteries of Sinai and just dump them in the land. Those
commandments of Sinai must be translated and restated, and if need
be, explicated and made pertinent.

Deuteronomy is a *long look back* to the model land of Genesis 1—2.
Deuteronomy is also a *knowing look across* the Jordan into the land.
The land does things for folks. This much Israel knew. The land will
rob one of hope, for everything is already given. And where all is
given, hope is troublesome.[48] The land will *rob one of memory.* Things
have been this way so long, we cannot remember when they were
different. The land will *rob one of neighbor,* for it is hard to care when
coveting works so well (cf. Joshua 7). The land will *rob one of the
mystery of God,* for other gods, though less awesome, can give rain.
When one is robbed of past and future, set in timelessness, when one
is robbed of God and neighbor, there is only "I" remaining. Then
life becomes short and empty and barbarous. Moreover, just possibly,
life shall be "required" in the night (cf. Luke 12:20). So education in
this ethos is concerned about the land.

But Deuteronomy will concede nothing. This part of the Torah
holds the passionate conviction that one can live timefully with hope
and faith in the land. Deuteronomy is the assertion that one can live
toward God and for neighbor in the land; it is the claim that the land
is not decisive for the shape of existence. Even in the land, Israel will
not deny its calling. So there is a call to remember. Only remembering will keep Israel in its calling. So our "teaching exchanges" with
which we have begun, between children and adults, is not only an
urging to remember. They are the very practice of remembering.
Remembering gives Israel power for a faithful life in a context of
accommodation. The Torah intends that when the children engage in
this exchange, they will be offered a new world in which to live—not,
however, a negotiable world. This new world is given, and it is there
to enter. It is a given world in which Israel has to do with Yahweh,
even as Yahweh has to do with Israel:

> I will take you for my people, and I will be your God; and you shall
> know that I am the Lord your God, who has brought you out from
> under the burdens of the Egyptians (Exod. 6:7).

The narrative ends with the affirmation undoubted, but at a point
of uneasiness. The promises have not yet been kept. They are
undoubted and unfulfilled. From the beginning, from Gen. 2:15–17,
the question has been the same as it is in Deuteronomy: How do we
receive the land and how do we live in it with the reality of vocation,
gift, prohibition?

The Torah of Israel is very sure about its main claims. It does not
argue or prove. It simply asserts. The Torah provides the grounds for
solidarity and consensus in the community. It is the foundation from
which all other matters derive. But that solidarity and consensus has
a peculiarly internal quality which assures that the scandalous particularity of this community is never to be accommodated to the large
community. Thus turned *inward*, there is *solidarity*.[49] All of us in
Israel believe this narrative and take it as our truth. Turned *outward*,
there is *abrasion* because the peculiar holiness of this God leads to a
very peculiar ethos that the world does not value and cannot
embrace. It is an obedience rooted in memories of oppression and
liberation. It is an obedience aimed at a new future for widows and
orphans. Memories of oppression and liberation, dreams of com-
forted widows and cared-for orphans—that is a consensus for any day,
but a consensus sure to be under attack.

The question always must be asked again as Israel engages in its
memory. What do these stones mean? They mean that we proceed in
an odd history with alternative roots and with alternative hopes. And
the odd, awkward ritual[50] of these stones announces to the rulers of
this age that we will keep practicing our awkward memories and our
abrasive hopes in every season and in the face of every alternative.

3
The Disruption
for Justice

A community which educates its members in the Torah will do them
a great service. It will make available a center for life, a core of memory, a focus around which to organize all of experience. But if a community educates only in the Torah, it may also do a disservice to its
members. It may nourish them to fixity, to stability that becomes
rigidity, to a kind of certitude that believes all of the important questions are settled. The answers need only to be recited again and again.

That is why alongside of the Torah, there is a second division of the
canon. This prophetic part of the canon consists of eight "books,"
the four former prophets—Joshua, Judges, Samuel, and Kings—and
the four latter prophets—Isaiah, Jeremiah, Ezekiel, and the Twelve.
When we come to the second part of Israel's canon, it is clear that we
face a very different *mode of knowledge* and a very different *substantive
claim*. In Jer. 18:18, our "presenting text," the second element in a
general summary of Israel's authoritative teaching is "the word from
the prophet." As is well known among us, the word of the prophet
stands in some contrast to the Torah of the priest. We have seen that
the Torah deals in that which is normative, known, and given. It
answers the child's question about who we are and what we are
about. The answer is already known and settled. The Torah reports
that on which there is a consensus. It is essentially uncritical or pre-
critical. It does not invite intellectual curiosity, penetration, or analysis. The Torah is not debatable. It states the basis on which analysis

and debate can take place. The Torah itself, however, is positioned to be beyond such questioning.

In contrast to all of that, the word of the prophet is something immediate, intrusive, and surprising. It is not normative. It is not known in advance. It is a way of knowledge that is not known until it is uttered. When it is uttered, its function may be to break the Torah, to challenge the consensus, to practice criticism on that which, until now, has been beyond criticism. Much recent scholarship has shown that the prophets depend on and are informed by the Torah.[1] There is an important dimension of *continuity* between the Torah and the prophets. This continuity is important for education and for the life of the church. A community illiterate of the Torah will not understand the prophet. But Zimmerli[2] has recently shown that the prophets use the Torah to argue against the Torah. They not only honor the Torah, but they mean to critique the Torah and move beyond it. Or to say it another way, the Torah is the "Yes" of God to Israel (2 Cor. 1:19). Yes, I will be your God. Yes, you are my people. Yes, I will be with you. The prophets add a critical footnote to all of this. "Yes, but what if . . ." Thus there is a tension between Torah and prophets which must always be attended to in education. The tension is between the dialectic of establishing or *asserting the consensus,* and then raising questions which break or challenge or *criticize the consensus* for the sake of a new word from the Lord. The two divisions (Torah/prophets) of the canon together suggest that education is the nurture of a restlessness with every old truth for the sake of a new truth which is just breaking upon us.

When we come to the prophetic materials, we are obviously in another world, a strange world. The text which gives us our title is an episode in Jer. 37:16–21. The narrative itself suggests a great deal about how we may understand prophecy. First, there is an encounter with the king at a time of great public crisis. That is when prophecy surfaces. The young king, Jehoiachin, has been exiled to Babylon. Armies are invading, just as Jeremiah said they would. The kingdom of Judah is in great danger. Zedekiah, the uncle of the young king, must now act as king, even though he is no king. As a regent or pretender, he is frightened, vascillating, intimidated, inept, unable to make a decision. He holds all the formal apparatus of power, undoubtedly including limousine and briefcase. But he knows he has no power to act in any way that will impact events. He has lost initiative. This is a characteristic reading of kings in the prophetic literature. Thus the narrative is not a neutral presentation, but in its structuring of the meeting, already makes a prophetic judgment. Kings, according to prophetic literature, are the embodiment of official power and public knowledge. But the prophetic literature is not terribly impressed with public definitions of reality. Kings must not be taken too seriously. Thus education in the prophetic means teaching folks not to take too seriously official truth about fact, knowledge, value, or power.[3]

The other party to this encounter is Jeremiah the prophet. He is not an impressive figure here. He had announced to any who would listen that the end was coming, the end of the life-world[4] so carefully constructed by kings in the interest of kings. Not only would Babylon destroy Judah, he said, but this destruction would happen because of Yahweh's will. God willed the destruction of his special people. How is that for flying in the face of the certitudes of the Torah? You only have I known of all the peoples of the earth (cf. Gen. 18:19). You only have I chosen; therefore . . . (Amos 3:2). The destruction plays from the Torah, but surely moves beyond it. In Jer 37:13-14, just before our passage, Jeremiah is imprisoned as a deserter. In 38:4, just after our passage, he is accused of treason. So here he is in a dungeon without power, influence, authority, or credentials. He is characteristically in trouble with the authorities. Among the authorities with whom he is in trouble are the teachers of the Torah.[5]

Being in trouble with the authorities need not mean public demonstrations in the streets, although it may mean that. But being in trouble is based in more elemental things, like the formation of an alternative imagination[6] that never ceases questioning the managers of the Torah, that never concedes ultimate authority to any public claim, and that never fully settles for the "official truth" of the realm.[7]

So there is an encounter between these two, the king who has no kingly initiative in his hands, and the prophet who is a dangerous person. But the strangeness is in this: the king comes to the prophet. That the king comes is no doubt terribly important, surely a bit of gloating irony on the part of the prophetic narrative. It is not that the prophet goes to confront the king (as with Elijah in 1 Kings 18:1). Here the prophet need only wait, for eventually the king will have played out his string. Eventually the king will have no alternative. The one with all the forms of power comes for help to this one who has none of the forms of power. There is in this narrative a radical and remarkable epistemological reversal which we will have to take seriously if we are to understand this second part of the canon. That the movement is from king to prophet is reminiscent of the awesome meeting of Yahweh with Abraham in Gen. 18:22. The narrator there is aware of the nuances of the meeting. The text as we now have it reports, as we might expect, "Abraham stood before the Lord." That is as we would expect it: human agent before the throne of God. But the scribal evidence is that in the earlier version of that text it said, "The Lord stood before Abraham." Imagine, the great God stood to be instructed by this father of faith! The text has been changed because the irony of that confrontation was too much to bear. In the analogous meeting in Jeremiah 37, however, the text has not been changed. Of course the person of God is not at issue. But the person and office and claim of the king are very much at issue. Now the king is clearly the suppliant.

The one who is supposed to know is the king. That is the function of the king. He has all the formal channels of intelligence. Yet he comes to this isolated one who has no claim to know anything. The entire narrative (and both parties accept the point) is that knowledge for the crisis is not given in normal channels and by regular means. Pertinent knowledge is given in ways we would rather not. The "old truth" over which the king presides is not adequate for the crisis. The "new word" now needed is not easily administered.[8] It does not conform to the definitional world of the king. There is no reliable one-to-one correlation between the *structures of society* and the *in-breaking of new truth from God.* That is the most important critical

aspect of this part of the canon. It is hard for us to take. Yet everything is at stake in this claim. We are accustomed to think that there is
some match-up between the *substance of truth* and the *structures of
authority.* The better off we are, educationally and economically, the
more we like to rely on the match. So we expect religious leaders to
know about the handling of sin. We expect doctors to know most
about illness and health. We count on government leaders to know
most about such embarrassments as Vietnam. And we do believe that
somewhere, if we can find them, there are consultants who know the
best truth about every problem. The decent ordering of society
depends on willingness to credit the authorities with having authority
and access to reliable information. When that linkage gets ques-
tioned, then everything is at risk. That is what is happening in this
dramatic meeting. The leader of the *authority structure* no longer has
access to the *truth.*

How dramatic and how subversive it is for the king to come to the
prophet. He came *secretly.* The text says, "in hiddenness." Of course
he did, like Nicodemus at night (John 3:2). He did not make a public
pilgrimage to get advice. He managed to keep his public form intact.
But by his coming, he conceded everything to the prophet. That,
then, is the claim of this part of the canon—that the public, official
ways to life finally cannot deliver. We must await *unadministered disruption.* The disruptions are unpleasant and unwelcome, but they are
the only hope we have in a society hellbent to death.

So the king came with the one question he dare not ask and remain
king. "Is there any word from the Lord?" The king now comes as
supplicant. The traitor is now recognized as the source of saving
knowledge. The prophet must have enjoyed the scene at long last. He
is justifiably coy. He says, "There is." There must have been a pause
at that point, a long pause. The prophet knows. The king does not
know. The literature savors this moment of deep inversion. The king
has all the apparatus of knowledge and knows everything except what
he needs to know. Normative, public knowledge is like a fabric of lies
fashioned by "the best and the brightest,"[9] or like the assurances of
the scientists just before the break of Three Mile Island.

In the exchange which happens in the text, two things are asserted. First, it is Yahweh who causes things to happen, not Zedekiah or Judah or Babylon or Egypt. The official versions of public life are finally irrelevant. The empty-handed posture of the king is a delegitimating of every earthly authority. The ones charged with knowing do not know. Imagine having that in the canon! Imagine teaching it in the church. Every form of human knowledge and human power is provisional. Second, the narrative asserts that Jeremiah, the imprisoned traitor, has access to Yahweh's intent. He is a nobody whom the king thought he had disposed of. But Jeremiah is not so readily disposed of. In this drama the king is seen to be no king. He cannot do what must be done to rule. He does not *know*. He cannot *decide*. He must go hat (crown?) in hand to the prophet. So we are at a summit meeting between the powerful king who is powerless and the powerless prophet who has power over the realm. The first here are embarrassingly the last, and the last first. The humbled one is exalted. The exalted one is humbled. And there is a claim here about knowledge and modes of knowing.

At least three other incidents speak to our epistemological concern regarding the same surprise of new, liberating truth:

Gen. 41:1–18 Pharaoh cannot get his royal apparatus to interpret his dream. So he turns to Joseph who has no credentials.

Exod. 8:18 Moses and Aaron do what imperial technicians in Egypt cannot do.

John 3:1–15 As already mentioned, Nicodemus, a teacher of the Jews, is confronted by the new teaching of Jesus, but only at night.

In each of the three cases, the prophetic figure bears a new word. He offers a radical, disruptive act or statement which supersedes the old order now delegitimated. In prophecy we are dealing with a *new truth* when the *old truth* controlled by human power has grown irrelevant, weary, and boring. The new truth each time places all the old truth and all the old truth manages in jeopardy. E. Jüngel describes truth as "interruption in the continuity of life."[10] The prophets

appear when the old consensus is at the brink of failure. They assert
that the old structures of human reason and human management are
obsolete because of the new thing now wrought by God. Surely Zedekiah would not have sought out Jeremiah if he had any alternative to
the humiliating request. Though on a much grander scale, it is like
driving around lost in a strange city, but preferring to hunt in desperation, rather than to ask someone who might know. That the king
asks is a measure of his desperation. Zedekiah or any king would look
a long time rather than ask.

Paul Lehmann has illuminated the encounter of Jesus and Pilate in
John 18:33—19:18.[11] In fact it is Pilate and not Jesus on trial. It is the
old truth of the empire placed in jeopardy by the new truth who is as
"one with authority." Pilate is made to say, "What is truth?" (18:38).
That is the surprising epistemological crisis, when the governor of
official, imperial truth no longer knows. I submit that our time is
such a time for a staggering prophetic moment. It is clear that the old
truth in our world has failed. While these examples from the Bible
are easily drawn from the realm of politics, the same dangerous critique must be turned on our best religious knowledge as well. This
education urges that we consider the failure of old truth and the
surprise and authority of new, disruptive words.

NEW REVELATION AND
POETIC RATIONALITY

So we begin with the first of our two questions, the *mode of knowledge*. How does Israel know in the prophetic word? What is the process that seems to function in the disruptive word? What processes
are to be taught out of this part of the canon about ways of knowing?
From our test in Jeremiah 37, we do not learn very much. So let me
make these observations about prophetic epistemology.

1. The knowing of the prophets must surely concern *psychology*.[12] A
lot of ink has been spilled on that question and a great deal of com-
parative material is available. But we cannot be very precise. What
we can say is that the prophets were not simply bold, rational observers. They were persons who could be impinged upon by spiritual

power that lay *outside the rationality of their culture.* Stated in phenomenological terms, they were open to "the spirit world." Stated in Israel's own categories, they could be influenced by the live word of God. In any case, they received and therefore announced certitudes and experiences which others did not share. The reception of such a certitude was a convulsive experience, probably as convulsive to their rationality as to their psyche. They were seized, grasped, raped, seduced, confiscated, gripped by realities that broke epistemological conventions. While it appears that in its earlier form some of this could be simulated or induced (1 Sam. 10:9–13; 19:18–24), the main testimony is that the source of such experience is a mystery beyond the ones involved. That is, the new confrontation is a genuine intrusion, not a contrivance.

Now such data admits of more than one reading. If one wants to discredit the prophets, one can say they are religious freaks or weirdos, that what they say must be assessed "considering the source." That is, discredit the means, and then the content can also be dismissed. But psychology does not need to accept such conventional criteria. It is also possible to conclude the prophets operated with a *sense of reality* that lay *outside royal rationality.* They did not accept the presumptive world of the dominant culture. They refused to have their knowledge or perception or imagination limited to or controlled by such social constraints. So one may say the prophets are *crazy* (cf. Hos. 9:7). Or one may say they are *free.* The relation of being *crazy* and *free* is difficult to assess. Much depends on one's own setting in making a judgment. The imagination of the prophets left them open to experiences, discernments, and disruptions that were denied in principle by convention. Church education is not intended to make people crazy, but it is to nurture people in an openness to alternative imagination which never quite perceives the world the way the dominant reality wants us to see it.

It is clear, in any case, that the "psychology of the prophets" cannot be understood simply as a personal psychological experience, but must take into account social definitions of reality. To treat the "psychology of the prophets" only as personal psychology is to assume that the definitional world lies beyond criticism. Such a break with rationality, however, implies a sharp criticism of that very rationality.[13]

2. Psychology as it is usually handled in the prophets is a modern phenomenon. The Bible itself does not move in these modes, but is much more likely to approach the same matters *mythologically.* We may leave open the question of whether the modern move from *mythology to psychology* is a responsible one. For our purposes, it is important to recognize the dominant mythological construct in the prophets which is especially evident in Jeremiah. That construct is the claim of having been involved with the divine council of the gods,[14] summoned to transmit their messages and authorized with the authority of the divine decree. All of this, it is usually held, is presumed in the legitimating formula, "Thus saith the Lord."[15] That is, the prophet does not speak his/her own word, but speaks for the royal government of heaven.

Now we may find that mythological construct difficult and far from our experience. However, if we take it not as a *religious,* but as a *political* claim, it is then close to our experience. The term "myth" does not refer to an absolute truth, but to an alternative political claim that is postured as nonnegotiable. Messengers do carry messages not their own. That is how every governmental emissary works. The difficulty for us is the claim that there is a decision-making agent (God, divine council) to which we do not have access and which is neither a projection of ourselves nor completely beholden and responsive to us. That is, the offense of this prophetic construct is not in its *mythical trappings,* but in the *substantive claim of the freedom of God.*

Such a mythological claim was offensive to Israelite kings and is, of course, offensive to all persons with power. Such persons always imagine that the real decisions are in their competence and are always made in their presence and under their supervision. The "myth" of divine council, then, has a political, polemical function. For it is clear that the real decisions are made elsewhere, beyond the reach of the king and in the absence of the king. Consequently, this mode of

knowledge argues in the direction of providence and destiny, and in
the direction of decisions to which we are *object* and not *subject*. That
is an exceedingly important educational theme in a culture which
imagines that we are present to all decisions and have all the data, and
that finally we will be the subject of all active verbs. The prophetic
claim is a challenge to the false view that we are lords of the world
and that the world is our creature. The "myth" of divine council is a
poetic way of grounding authority so that it lies beyond the reach of
the king.

My impression is that Martin Luther King, Jr. has most effectively
appealed to such authority in recent time. Both in his speech, "I have
a dream,"[16] and in his last public statement, "I have been to the
mountain,"[17] he made his appeal to an epistemology that lies beyond
the conventions of our culture. His reason for doing this was to
ground his claims beyond and outside the conventions of racism. In
ancient or modern world, such an appeal may not be right. But it is
by definition unarguable, even though Jeremiah did argue about it.

3. A third facet of the way of prophetic knowledge is to pay attention to the *sociology of the prophets*.[18] This is a relatively neglected and
new question, one that surely warrants increased attention. Since the
work of Mannheim in the sociology of knowledge,[19] it is clear that
everyone's epistemology is in part determined by social context, that
is, by the reality of economic and political status and power, or the
lack thereof. Habermas's title, *Knowledge and Human Interests*,[20] goes
further in suggesting how intimately tied together are *knowledge* (both
how we know and what we know) and a variety of *vested interests*.

Much more attention has been given to prophetic *psychology* than
to prophetic *sociology*. (That in itself is a sociological statement of
some importance.) Nevertheless, we may identify two efforts concerning sociology. First, using methods of contemporary sociology,
Peter Berger[21] has explored the question of whether the prophets can
be placed in the institutions of time. That is, can the prophets be
placed in the institutional life of Israel and yet criticize the institution? Second, in a very different way, Hans Walter Wolff[22] has paid
attention to the *Heimat* of the prophets. In a series of papers, Wolff

has proposed the social location of the prophets in a variety of settings. His most recent study of Micah[23] has gone farthest in understanding Micah in terms of his economic setting, as a leader of the
landed community of elders in conflict with the usurpation power of
the royal enterprise.

The payoff of both Berger and Wolff is to suggest that the prophets
are not contextless voices. They are nurtured in and sustained by a
community of some kind. Wilson argues that the prophets of Israel
tend to be the voices of "peripheral communities,"[24] peripheral in
terms of social power, and therefore peripheral in terms of religious
perception. The prophets not only live in but are shaped and
instructed by the life of such communities. What is offered as the
word of the Lord is often not far removed from the *passionate agenda of
the community.* In this way there is an intimate linkage between a
clear *political agenda* and the *theological claim* of God's word. The
prophet speaks God's alternative word, which stands free from and
over against the dominant community. That free word, however, is
better understood as reflective of a community not fully contained by
the royal rationality. There is a surprising affinity between the *word
of Yahweh* and the *community of the marginal ones* in which the
prophet lives and from which he/she speaks.[25]

This is a most important resource for education. Though it may be
educationally difficult, an important implication is that the texts we
regard as authoritative and canonical are in fact marginal in their
origin and claims. Education may require reexperiencing that kind of
marginality both in terms of social power and in terms of rationality.
We have not done very well in utilizing sociological learning or in
urging appropriate sociological "suspicion." Or against that, we may
incline to some contextless word of the Lord. But Wilson makes a
strong case that the live word of the Lord is congenial to the cries and
disruptions coming from the peripheral communities. This mode of
study urges a realism about prophetic texts which stays closely linked
to human realities.

4. Closely related to the sociological aspects of the prophets, but
more congenial to Scripture study in the past, is the location of the
prophets in terms of Israel's *religious institutions and traditions.* A

phase of scholarship recently stressed has insisted that the prophets can only be understood as children of Israel's life and faith. On the one hand, this means that the prophetic word appeals to the traditions of Israel, especially to the commandments and the Mosaic traditions of "mighty deeds."[26] On the other hand, and in a more narrow way, the prophets are understood as agents of public worship, being actually ordained officers of the cult.[27] This argument would hold that the critical, liberated voice of the prophets is not a surprise in Israel, but is constitutive for Israel. These two points then are an argument which *links the prophets to the Torah.* If the prophets are officers of the covenant-making institution and are bearers of the tradition, they are very much heirs and children of the Torah. The relation of Torah and prophets is a delicate one. There are aspects of continuity and discontinuity; both appeal to the consensus and a shattering of the consensus.

All of these elements—psychological, mythological, sociological and institutional—are important in seeing that the prophets are not lone, isolated figures whose authoritative word comes out of private spiritual experience. That is, the prophetic, the prophetic literature, and the prophetic canon are all to be understood as *definitional for the community.* As the texts now stand, the prophets are not an extra that happened to be tagged on to the Torah as an incidental extra. Rather, it is argued that the prophets are constitutive and definitional for this community of faith. They are as crucial for a proper understanding of Israel as is the Torah, though obviously in a quite different way. Education which is faithful to this division of the canon must nurture people to sense that this community of faith is a natural home and a proper arena for the voice of shattering which violates the consensus.

That leads us to our main point on prophetic epistemology. We cannot finally focus on the *persons* of the prophets, because that largely eludes us. Moreover, we are not trying to get behind the text, but to understand what is going on in the text. Therefore our attention is to the prophetic literature. What is given there is a form of knowledge. It is the *literature* rather than the *personality* which ought to concern us.

The most important point to observe is that the prophets are *poets.*

Prophetic speech is characteristically poetic speech. The importance of this cannot be overstated. The prophets are not political scientists with blueprints for a social order. They are not crusaders for a cause. They are not ethical teachers. They are speakers (not writers) who commit linguistic acts that assault the presumed world of the king, who expose the pretensions of the royal system, and who invite listening Israel to entertain new dimensions of social possibility which they had never before considered. The prophets (in much of Protestantism) have been mistakenly understood as social activists or as social reformers. But they have the more fundamental task of nurturing poetic imagination.[28] By this capacity to draw new pictures, form new metaphors, and run bold risks of rhetoric, they create a new arena for Israel's imagination and derivatively for Israel's political actions. They seek to form an alternative context for humanness by creating a different presumptive world which is buoyed by different promises, served by different resources, sobered by different threats, and which permits different decisions. That is the visible result of this liberated imagination which goes public in Israel. It does not matter greatly if this liberated imagination is justified by an alternative psychology, a polemical mythology, a protesting sociology, an authorizing institutionalization, or a combination of these factors. As we face the text, what counts is that the prophets' speech, artistic skill, rhetorical courage, emotional sensitivity, and political "hutzpah" all stand free of the dominant conventions—free to protest against, free to disclose change, free to move on to better worlds.[29]

The greatest threat to the prophetic canon, either in the ancient world or in our education, is to have poetic oracles from the prophets reduced to prose. It is like having great art diminished to technique or great music "explained." Prose is always the language of the king, of the "managerial mentality."[30] If the prophet can be reduced to prose, then the *message* can be translated into a *program*. And the program, predictably, will be administered by the same people who administer everything else.

The poetry of the prophets serves three purposes:

1. Its very idiom breaks and shatters the dominant universe of discourse. Its very expression critiques royal rationality. The poet gets

away with dangerous things as long as his poetry is impressionistic. Such expression refuses to be reduced to a program because the prophetic intent is not to critique royal programs, but the entire presumptive world of the king. Thus the very practice and nurture of poetic imagination is itself a prophetic enterprise. Persons who are nurtured into irony, metaphor, and parable are persons who are likely to maintain some critical distance from every managed world.[31]

2. The intent of prophetic poetry is to take Israel *inside* the life-experiences which might be treated *externally* as only ethical or political. That is, poetry has the time and the patience as well as the impatience to pay attention to the textures and nuances of experience, to notice the rawness and terror, the emptiness and surprise which belong to historical experience. This poetry refuses to let life be quantified, generalized, summarized. It insists on taking time to notice the human dimensions of pain and healing. It dares to give cosmic proportion to these aspects of life, claiming that the texture of human suffering and human healing is a match for what happens in the heart of God. The prophets believe and assert that the worst scandal is not to notice the grief and delight that are at the bottom of the world, in the heart of God. The rhetoric which portrays these scenes from "the other side" is a gamble that if Israel can be led to discern what transpires in the heart of God through this story of hope and betrayal, Israel might learn something important about its own life. Thus the prophetic poetry is a protest against every reduction of life from its rawness, from life being lived rather than merely passed through. That intent makes a special claim on the life of Israel as a bearer of truth. But that claim itself rests on a claim about God, who is the Lord of hope and hurt.

3. The prophets, however, are not poets who are simply fascinated with words or with the emotional aspects of life. There is a relation between their rhetoric which presages new worlds and their hunch about God's will. The literary/rhetorical enterprise is not an end in itself, though the prophets clearly work toward prophetic sensitivity. This poetry is informed by a two-world construct, a tension of continuity and discontinuity between the present world and the promised world. With some exceptions[32] this poetry seems to reflect the world

of the have-nots, who know deeply that they have been promised
more than they have been permitted. The promise is from God, the
permit is from the present managers. But this language believes the
full promise will outlast the niggardly permit. This is partisan,
polemical poetry which means *to buoy* those who might otherwise
quit, and *to assault* those who will not care. So the poets engage in
fantasy. Their fantasy, however, is fixed on the realities of social
power and social possibility. They reject any romantic poetry which
sounds religious, but which never touches the shames and hopes of
power in the world. Their *language* (which breaks the rational,
administered consensus) is linked to their *social hope* (which subverts
present power arrangements). We have a great deal of work to do in
the church on the political function of language, on the capacity of
language to legitimate or delegitimate configurations of power.

So the question of Zedekiah to Jeremiah still awaits an answer: "Is
there a word from the Lord?" Are there those with liberated tongues
and passionate dreams that well up the rhetoric of certitude within
them, the voice of newness that breaks out and shatters? It must not
be just a voice of anger, though it may be that. Rather, it must be a
voice which will stand on the text of the very consensus it shatters.
The question will not be answered unless there is a match between a
voice of eloquence and a *new truth of a world ending and beginning.*
The good tongue will not be wasted on an old tired truth. The new
world will not be given without a tongue to speak it into existence.
The educational task of the community is to nurture some to prophetic speech. But for many others, it is to nurture an awareness that
we must permit and welcome and evoke that prophetic tongue among
us. Otherwise we will be diminished into the prose world of the king
and, finally, without hope. Where there is no tongue for new truth,
we are consigned to the coldness of the old truth.

ENDINGS AND BEGINNINGS
BEYOND THE POSSIBLE

The *substantive* issue posed by the second part of the Old Testament canon concerns the *possibility of new truth* in the community of

faith. When we considered the Torah, we concluded that Torah education is to nurture persons in the deepest, most reliable truth. That is, adults give answers to children's questions which are well known and commonly believed among us. But now we have an educational task that seems to fly in the face of that: the nurture of persons in readiness for and expectant of new disruptions *which violate the old consensus of disclosure.* The staging is in a *word* which comes as a surprise. It is a word of passion, but a word that has substance. It is a word which claims an external authority. Most of all it is a free, irreverent, unaccommodating word. It refuses to accommodate the perception or epistemology of present power arrangements. It is a word that violates conventional expectations and conventional legitimations—a word which not only sounds strange to the children, but is unknown to the adults until it is spoken (cf. Deut. 8:3). It is a word which breaks every reality upon which we rely.[33]

When we ask about the "what" of prophetic speech, we have some deciding to do. Some scholars believe that the main word of the prophets is a call to *repentance.*[34] That squares with popular notions of the prophets as speakers of righteous indignation. Moreover, while it has all the sting of passion to it, a call to repentance is in fact a holding action, calling people back to "the old truth." It is as though everything is in fact in order. There is simply a need for wayward ones to return to *that order.* Without denying the presence of the motif of repentance, I should urge that repentance is a marginal notion in the prophets.[35] For such a view assumes Yahweh is fixed, and only God's people must change. But that is not the "what" of the prophets:

1. The motif does not occur that often.[36]

2. It is, in fact, a way of domesticating the prophets, that is, it leaves them in "a known world" and tends to be didactic. Thus kings can repent without changing things at bottom. An emphasis on repentance may be *didactic,* but it is scarcely *kerygmatic.*[37]

3. Repentance places everything in human hands. That is, things will be better if human persons act right.[38] I submit that such an emphasis is not wrong, but is too tame for the main thrust of this

section of the canon. It is as though the prophets mainly speak about human activity, as though God were simply a fated appendix which follows automatically on human goodness or evil. An evangelical reading of the prophets cannot accept that kind of reduction.

So let us try in another direction. Of course it is problematic to try to reduce this liberating poetry. It does not admit of summary. But we may suggest that Jer. 1:10 serves as an epitome for the "new truth" of these poets:

> See, I have set you this day over nations and over kingdoms,
> to pluck up and to break down,
> to destroy and to overthrow,
> to build and to plant.

There are two sets of verbs here. On the one hand, there are four verbs of negativity: pluck up/break down/destroy/overthrow. They suggest that God is *bringing an end to the world as we have known it.* God is bringing an end to a world we very much want not to end and really believe cannot end. The other verbs, "build and plant," bear witness to the *evocation of a new world*—one that did not previously exist, one that we did not believe could come to be, and one from which we flinch at its coming. So the substance of the work of the prophets revolves around these six verbs. In one form or another, they are prominent in the speech of Jeremiah.[39]

Less directly, it may be argued that these verbs also comment on what the other prophets are about. In this and the preceding verse (Jer. 1:9–10), it is claimed not only that *God terminates and evokes,* but that the capacity and authority to do this has now been *entrusted to the poet:* "I have put my words in your mouth. . . ."[40] This speaker speaks "the new truth" that brings the new situation. The new truth is the end of worlds we cherish and the beginning of worlds we do not fully welcome. In both cases, the new truth violates the old truth to which we are committed. For the old truth assumed and affirmed that the world was sure.[41] The adults knew the answers in that old world. "Old truth" upholds "old world." New truth threatens that old world.

Now such a summary is of course risky business. It is like reducing a good painting to a cliché. I take courage to do that because Clements[42] has suggested that this way of summarizing is already going on in the text itself. It is the canonical process within the Bible itself that understands the prophets in terms of these motifs. Notice how much more radical this is than a call to repentance. It is an argument that the real issues do not finally concern human action, human guilt, or human repentance. The prophets' concern is God's way with the world. While God's actions are aimed at Israel, they are not controlled by Israel. God is clearly an independent, liberated agent whose actions run beyond Israel's capacity for control or even expectation. That is heady stuff for education, if educators want to focus on human responsibility as an end in itself.

1. The prophetic claim is this: *The old known world is coming to an end.* It will be clear why Zedekiah had to go to Jeremiah for this word. It will be clear why this shattering word comes to prophet and not to king. And it will be clear why kings are predictably hostile to prophets who speak such a word. The task of the king is, by official charge and most likely by inclination, to assure continuity of the known world. That is, kings preside over and rely upon the consensus that this world is the one we have had and do have and will have. There is no other world except this one. The king's business is to nurture and manage that consensus and to keep it intact.[43] About this world, kings must always make the affirmation, "as it was in the beginning, is now and ever shall be, world without end." Kings embody and represent the endurance of the present, the eradication of a different past, and the prohibition of a different future.[44] I suggest that this central substance of the second part of the canon poses an urgent and difficult educational task since adherence to the royal consensus is much valued among us. This part of the canon offers a programmatic violation of that consensus. Any education which purports to be seriously biblical must explore this dangerous challenge to the consensus.[45]

Kings cannot imagine that the present can ever end. The present life-world is the frame of royal responsibility. To think without the present configuration of power and order and norms is to invite anarchy. I do not know how radically to understand this business about the end of the known world. When we speak of its end, we are likely talking not about the physical world, but the life-world, the social universe in which we live and on which we rely. But in the fray, we cannot separate these kinds of worlds. When our life-world is threatened, it is surely discerned as the end of the world. What the second part of the canon must speak about is the end of the world—life-world or any known world. To kings, ancient and modern, reality cannot be conjured outside this world. That is the danger and deepness of this part of the canon—the rhetorical freedom to imagine a world not shaped the way we experience its shape. Such a prospect lies beyond us in our need to control.

Those of us who think about the prophetic canon are likely also to be enmeshed in the royal consciousness. We think like kings; our interests tend to be more with Zedekiah than with Jeremiah. This complicates the educational processes urged by this section of the canon. We trust the known world. We operate on its assumptions and value them. So we have no "we-they" situation, at least as concerns us. This subversive literature, then, stands over against all of us. In saying that, and in recognizing how kings resist the end of the known world, we should not miss the vested interest at work on the part of protective kings. Partly, it is a psychological impossibility to think outside the present system. But it is also the fact of being co-opted by the goodies. Never is it the outsider who thinks that the present is eternally ordained. So there is a neat convergence between *self-interest* and *passionate royal faith*. As the prophet announces the end, his/her rhetoric penetrates and challenges both the self-interest and the passionate faith of the royal holding action. The prophetic section of the canon is so hard to take because we all resist the end of the world, if indeed it happens to be our world. It is odd but unarguable that all of us become less radical, less prophetic, less noble about endings, the closer they draw to our own shop. That is why the prophets evoke so much hostility.[46] The known world cannot tolerate speech about the end of our world.

The end of the old known world is a preoccupation of the

prophets. The ninth-century prophets (that is, especially Elijah and Elisha) function to delegitimate kings, to show they are no kings. So they deny them power. More explicitly, from the eighth century, it is Amos 8:2 which articulates the end in communal categories.[47] Especially Jeremiah in the seventh century broods about and finally must speak about the end. Jeremiah reached the conclusion that even the holy city (and with it the entire royal apparatus) must be given over to the hands of the enemy. So Jeremiah is driven to exasperation, to grief, and finally to a desire to escape it all (Jer. 9:1-3). Jeremiah, who comes near the end of that prophetic thrust, articulates the collapse of all reliable institutions and delegitimates all authority. Only a shade beyond Jeremiah is Ezekiel in the sixth century. Together Jeremiah and Ezekiel experience the nullity of Israel.[48] Sometimes the prophets *anticipate*, sometimes they *warn* against, sometimes they *evoke* the end. Each time they require Israel to ponder the nullification of the known world, they make clear to God's people that ultimacy may not be assigned to my life-world no matter how hedged about it may be by sacred ideology. The end of the known world bespeaks a provisional quality of all of life when set before the throne of God.

2. The prophetic claim is this: *God is bringing a new world into being in the midst of the ruin and rubble of the old world.* The prophets are clear that none other than God has the freedom, power, and authority to cause to be a new world that did not exist until freshly given by God's speech and action. So there is a building and a planting for which there is no ground in the old world now gone. Perhaps this affirmation is an even more difficult and more scandalous proclamation than the negative point. The unexpected and powerful *graciousness* of God is more of an affront than even the *judgment* of God.

This scandal of prophetic speech is received by the kings not only as an impossibility, but as a threat. For it clearly endangers all royal definitions of what is possible. It undoes even the regnant definition of death. Kings in Israel are like all of us who look for a familiar shape in new actions. We tend to listen to new words until we catch something to place it into a slot of the already known. Then it will be safely administered, requiring no risk, reduced to thoughts we have already thought and plans we have already devised. Conventional notions of novelty are in fact the moving of pieces around without any thought of an in-breaking, of a new emergence that goes beyond what is already administered.

The prophets of Israel/Judah, however, speak a word authorized by a very different God. As early as Nathan (2 Sam. 7:11–16), kingship is a deep newness rooted only in God's free graciousness. The prophets speak promises which are not extrapolated from what has been before.[49] As von Rad has shown,[50] it is especially Jeremiah, Ezekiel and Second Isaiah who speak a staggering newness just at the point of nullity. They speak a newness which will not be contained in old categories. Thus the tradition of Jeremiah concerns a new covenant which is both like and unlike the old covenant (31:31–34). Ezekiel concerns the overcoming of death in Israel (37:1–14) and the surprise of the new temple (40—48). Second Isaiah speaks of a homecoming beyond every legitimate anticipation and stakes out freedom for God whose thoughts and plans are discontinuous with all those of human possibility (55:6–9). In establishing the distinctiveness of God's newness and its contrast to human imagination, Second Isaiah pursues a theme at which Hosea has already hinted (11:9). God is not human. God does not work as a human. Therefore God's capacity for newness fits none of our categories or definitions of "the possible."[51]

So this section of the canon suggests the emergences of new futures beyond our categories of expectation. That is a difficult agenda for education. It is here that education which is biblical must break with every parallel educational enterprise. There is "a planting and a building" which matches and over-matches the "tearing down" and the "plucking up" about which we have spoken. *There is a hopelessness* at the null point.[52] And *there is graciousness* precisely at the null point. This radical turn poses the question for educators. It is not an educational question first of all about how to teach. Nor is it a psychological question of being open to such an affirmation. The question is in fact about God and God's capacity to work newness. So Jeremiah, the one who knows most about the ending, is also the one who speaks most about the "turning of destiny" (29:14; 30:18; 31:23;

32:44; 33:7, 11, 26)[53] which is wrought by nothing other than the miracle of God. God has a plan for people, a plan of well-being (Jer. 29:11). This plan is not linked to or dependent upon human resolve (Isa. 55:8-9). The resolve of God will not be resisted by any other agent in heaven or on earth (Isa. 14:24-27).

The prophetic canon thus revolves around great movements of ending and beginning, of dying and new life, of suffering and hope, of lament and doxology. These are the rich and multifaceted themes of Jer. 1:10. We find that the moves—to pluck up and to tear down, to plan and to build—are in fact both scandalous and unacceptable. Both are thought to be impossible. Both violate our royal rationality. Both shatter our control. Therefore both are resisted, not only as actuality, but as possibility.

Both *the end* and the *new beginning* are regarded as "too hard" for God to do. The prophetic task, then, is to speak about what is too hard, what violates the consensus and goes beyond the public expectations of Israel. Both are impossible—that Israel (or the Messiah) should die and that Israel should be made new (or that the Messiah should be raised from the dead). The dialectic of both kinds of impossibility is found in the statement of Jer. 32:17-27, a prose passage derived from the memory of the prophet. On the one hand, the use of "too hard" in v. 27 concerns the end of the known world. Israel did not believe it could happen. In v. 17 the same word is used in relation to the command of v. 25 to invest in the land that will be rebuilt. In v. 27 the impossibility is the end. In v. 17, the impossibility is the new beginning. Both appear "too hard,"[54] yet both are affirmed by the prophet. This prophet, and indeed the whole prophetic canon, is engaged in a dispute over what is possible. The old consensus had articulated what was known to be possible. Now the prophet joins issue with those articulations of the possible. This part of the canon challenges old definitions of the possible and the impossible. It utilizes radical speech to evoke new realities. The new realities brought to speech run beyond what old Israel either hoped or feared.

3. It becomes clear that the intent of the prophetic canon is essentially to *disrupt* the *old censensus*. The community had probed and

shaped and stabilized the precious disclosure from the tradition. Over a period of time even the radical revelation of the tradition became fixed and settled and administered. It became stable enough so that any adult knew the right answer to the question of the child. There is a quality of "you have heard it said of old." The problem is that what was said of old had become a settled formula to define and legitimate a closed, settled world. So the Torah, taken by itself, has its radicality domesticated. Therefore there was need for an explosive, disruptive, "But I say unto you" that both *derived from* and *moved against* the old tradition.

For all of its probing of psychology and sociology, scholarship has not been able to "explain" the source of this radical speech in the second part of the canon. It will not be "explained" now any more than it could be explained at its happening. It is in fact *a new revelation* which surprises, shatters, violates, and offends. In the face of new revelation, our usual procedures for explaining do not work. The educational agenda is to teach and probe the authority of new revelation which flies in the face of old revelation, and to form a new community open to the claims of the new revelation.[55]

We need to be clear on how dangerous and unlikely new revelation is. Indeed, by definition new revelation is problematic. From where does it come? How can it be authenticated? It will not come from the legitimate managers of settled revelation, for example, the scribes (cf. Mark 1:21–28), because they are too busy guarding, defending, and interpreting the old revelation. They now sit in the "seat of Moses" (Matt. 23:2). They have fought and struggled to get to that seat. They are secure there and do not intend to vacate soon. So there is a nice match between sitting in the seat and the revelation that justifies having the seat and sitting in it. New revelation most likely will not come from those sources because inevitably the managers of the old revelation have a stake in the old revelation.[56] New revelation which questions this is threat; it is not good news.

Thus we are immediately pressed to recognize that new revelation must come from unlegitimated sources because there is a closed circle between old revelation and its proponents. That circle will be broken and shattered only by a new voice which has no such vested interest. That is, new truth is likely to be a *cry* from "below," not a *certitude* from "above." New truth from God is likely to come as a cry and a protest of the weak, the powerless, the disinherited ones. In the Old Testament, the new truth comes from among and on behalf of the widows and orphans, the ones trampled by conventional "justice." In our own time, it is the economically disinherited, the politically powerless, the ecclesiologically excluded who cry a new truth from God.

To take a case in point, from where is to come the claim for the ordination of women in the church? It is a cry which has to come from those who most feel the pain of exclusion. It is less likely, much less likely, to come from a male bishop (or seminary teacher) already safely ensconced as interpreter of the old revelation, the old truth. That is, new revelation must break through out of pain, exasperation, rage, incredulity, and irrationality[57] because the cry or the surprise means to break the rationality and shatter the universe of discourse that legitimates the present order.[58]

New truth in this prophetic canon is thus very much like *Catch-22.* If one speaks it, one flies against the old truth and by definition is wrong, excluded, and dismissed. Almost any new revelation will have to battle for legitimacy, beginning with the presupposition that new revelation which disrupts the old truth is illegitimate. The new truth will almost inevitably sound irreverent, disrespectful, and illegitimate. It will immediately be in conflict with revelation in the old consensus. The ones who so speak will be regarded either as crazy (cf. Hos. 9:7) or as treasonable (Amos 7:10–11; Jer. 38:4). So the second part of the canon creates a hard epistemological situation in the abrasion of old truth coming to terms with new truth. The educational question, then, is how to pick one's truth, how to know what is true among alternative truths. Such education is tricky because it means immediately placing in jeopardy the old consensus we have worked so hard to establish.

4. So how is the new truth as *disruption* to be received as *disclosure* from God?

First of all, in the Old Testament there are standard appeals to formal credentials. That is, presentations of new truth make the best case they can for what they say. This may appeal to agreement with the Torah. Thus Jer. 7:1–15 appeals to the *old tradition* of law to announce a radical risk for the community. Or there may be a formal appeal to a structure like *divine council* (this is the ground taken in Isa. 6:1–8 and the ground challenged in Jer. 23:18–22). Or, most frequently, there is appeal to the *authorizing formula,* "Thus saith the Lord." What an audacious claim! It is clearly not likely to carry great weight because it is a formula capable of use by any source, in good faith or not. The more it speaks against the old consensus, the less compelling it is likely to be.

Our reflection on prophetic authority is drawn finally beyond such extrinsic appeals to formula and construct, to intrinsic claims for what is said. One has a sense about such speech. It carries its own conviction and testimony as the voice of God. But notice what is being claimed in such an assertion, both by its claimants and by those who accept the claim. If the new truth is indeed from below, from the powerless ones or on behalf of the powerless ones, then it is implied that the *voice from below* is the *voice of God.* The cry of the weak ones is the cry of God. The surprise of a new thing on earth[59] is the work of the free God. The linkage, even the equation, is a bold and daring move which requires Israel to come outside the arena of conventional religion.

Implicit in the claim of prophetic authority is a particular characterization of God as the one who identifies with and sojourns among the marginal ones. (This is not at variance with the claims of the Torah—cf. Deut. 10:17–22—but the point is freshly made.) That is why the most poignant poetry comes out of the hurt of Hosea and Jeremiah, and the most radical prophetic hope comes out of the deepness of Second Isaiah. Thus one cannot move from the first to the second part of the canon without attending to the crisis in the character of God that comes with it. God is now asserted to be against the old consensus, as advocate for the marginal ones. God is asserted to be free to work a newness beyond the possibility of the old order. This is most obvious in the great classical prophets. But it is already evident in the ninth-century figures. Thus Elijah is a "troubler" in Israel (1 Kings 18:17) because he speaks the drought (17:1), because he cares for the widow (17:8–16), because he overcomes death (17:17–24). He brings a newness that violates royal definitions of life and death, of possibility and necessity.

Finally, we are driven to recognize the qualitatively different character of the second part of the canon. We have seen that the first part articulates the *ethos* of Israel and is characterized by solidity, certitude, consensus, and consolidation. Torah is a statement about belonging to Israel. It is not in doubt or in dispute. The second part of the canon moves away from such solidity of ethos to speak about the sharpness and wounded quality of *pathos*. Heschel[60] has urged that prophetic authority is rooted in God's pathos. The shatteredness of the prophets is reflective of God's own shatteredness. Or, said another way, new truth comes in the reality of suffering which engages the suffering of God. New hope arises only out of the reality of such suffering to nullification. The incredible pathos of the prophets—especially of Hosea, Jeremiah, and Second Isaiah—participates in God's own pathos. That is the only way new truth can come.[61]

Thus the intrinsic authority of these poetic statements is not that they confirm the same old conventional view of God, or that they echo the set answers adults give to children. Now they confront Israel with a new discernment of God. Here we have to do with a God who suffers and hurts, who aches and changes, who can be impinged upon. It is the way of kings to banish pathos, to shun suffering, to be immune to hurt, to deny those sensitivities. It is proper to the machismo of kings and queens to be above all such weakness. Gunkel has a marvelous phrase for this. He calls it a desire for "genuine discernment without suffering."[62] So the issue is joined—a conflict between old truth which is removed from passion and new truth with all the authority of weakness, hurt, and cry. The problem, of course, is that kings are immune to suffering and spend their time avoiding it. They do not believe endings or beginnings really happen. Therefore new truth that is shaped like suffering is received as "no truth."

It is a cry which must be silenced (Amos 7:12–13) or eliminated (Jer. 36:20–26).

The task of the second part of the canon is to bring the passion of God to speech—to speak in such ways of passion that the words will not be co-opted. To educate in this way is a heavy task. For the prophetic canon and all "new truth" from God is never disinterested. It is the voice of those who have given up on the old consensus, who know that God has promised much more than has been given. It is the conviction that more is to be given, if only the stranglehold of old truth can be broken. In our presenting scene of Jeremiah 37, the prophet says what must be said. Zedekiah, like all kings, does know how to respond. He doesn't like the new truth. But he does not doubt it either. So in 38:1–6, the king can't decide. Like Pilate with the other Bearer of new truth (John 19:1–11), Zedekiah surrenders this new voice to those who defend the old truth at any cost. The old truth has ways to deal with traitors and blasphemers. The second part of the canon, however, believes that things are never so fully or unambiguously resolved. The prophets may be routinely eliminated (Matt. 23:37), but the new truth will have its say.

4

The Discernment
of Order

The third division of the Old Testament Canon, the writings (*kethubim*), can hardly be spoken of as canon. That is true first because it is not a coherent body of literature as are the other two, but a miscellaneous collection. There is no agreement on the proper sequence of books, and the order varies from place to place. The second reason it is not properly a canon is that it does not seem to hold much authority. This is indicated by the free and sometimes careless way of translation. The very scribes who acted as fundamentalists in other parts of the Bible were not especially careful here. It is likely that before the New Testament period, this third section of the canon was known as an identifiable, relatively stable collection of writings.[1] Yet in a statement like that of Jesus on "the Torah and the prophets" (Matt. 22:40) the writings are at best peripheral and subordinate.

In any case, if one takes the trouble to consider the writings with some care, it is evident that there are important resources offered here. This literature makes available resources and perspectives on faith and knowledge that are not characteristic of the Torah or the prophets. That is, the third part of the canon has its own contribution to make to our topic. Of the diverse materials in this third part, our programmatic verse of Jer. 18:18 speaks about the "counsel of the wise."[2] Since that phrase is parallel to the "Torah of the priest" and the "word of the prophet," this may be an allusion to a third body of literature. It is at least a reference to a third way of knowledge and therefore a third aspect of Israelite epistemology and education. To be sure, "the counsel of the wise" does not comprehend the entire third part of the canon because other materials are there as well. But it points us to one important aspect of this literature, namely, the wisdom materials. That means first of all Proverbs, Job, and Ecclesiastes and, in the larger canon, Ben Sirach and the Wisdom of Solomon. It is clear that in the wisdom materials, even though they do not admit of reduction, we are dealing with a quite *didactic* frame of reference and epistemology. This material is the most self–consciously educational of any we have considered.

Because wisdom is such a problematic area, and because there has been a good bit of attention to it lately, some preliminary comments are in order:

1. Wisdom may no longer be treated as late and marginal in the Old Testament. It surely is to be found early and late as a serious *intellectual alternative* to the traditions that have been given most attention.

2. The evolutionary movement from secular to religious wisdom will not hold. Nor will any of the other developmental schemes from simple to complex, from ethically simple to theologically sophisticated. Rather, this is a rich and varied phenomenon which goes in many directions but which seems to have a common tendency in it. This is a widely held intellectual option that must have involved and appealed to many persons, including some of the best minds in that society.[3]

3. Wisdom in Israel needs to be understood as a serious way in which responsible, reasonable knowledge of the world and passionate trust in God are held together. We have here intellectually mature and theologically sensitive literature.[4] This is a believing reason, or we may say "faith seeking understanding." It is a different settlement of faith and reason than those that are given in the other literature, and therefore we should be attentive to it.

These are new and emerging judgments in scholarship.[5] Their importance for us is that they offer, even if somewhat ill-defined, a serious alternative attempt to be believers about the world. Therefore they claim our attention as educators.[6]

There are currently two main hypotheses about wisdom which we should take into account. I believe that we cannot choose between the hypotheses, for on different grounds, both have much to commend them. On the one hand, it is argued that there is *clan wisdom*,[7] the teaching of the young in a tribal community by an informal process of socialization. This kind of nurture was concerned with locating the parameters of safe and acceptable conduct and inculcating the governing values of the community in the next generation. This wisdom tried to identify what one may and may not do in the community. There are limits and boundaries to safe conduct. Wisdom also attends to the *dangers* of violating those limits. Some action may be dangerous because it invites visible *disaster*. Other actions are dangerous because they earn the *disapproval* of the community.[8] That is, "wrong" and "harmful" are not the same, but they are not unrelated. What earns the disapproval of the community may be experienced as social ostracism, or it may be the sanction of a religious taboo. Clearly such a nurture process aims heavily at social conformity,[9] but also at making people "street-wise," that is, able to cope and survive.

But this wisdom is not just attentive to danger. It includes also positive, practical, and concrete embodiment of "the way," of what we do in our community. Berger and Luckmann have shown that every community tends to make an easy move from *our way* to *the way*, that is, to forming absolutes derived from experience.[10] The community has learned some things by trial and error and knows something about getting along in the world.[11] This is the point of such nurture. The young do not need always to reinvent the wheel of morality, decency, and good judgment.

The other hypothesis is that wisdom reflects an actual school situation.[12] Wisdom is instruction in the *court school*. It aims at the nurture and discipline of upper-class boys who are born to power and destined to rule. Formal education, until recent time, was very much an elitist affair. Wisdom is instruction in the ways of power. There are parallels in this hypothesis to the great educators of the Renaissance, who served as tutors to children of the nobility. Now the issues of survival and coping are not at work, for all of that is assumed. But there are the issues of power and control, of *mastery, success, and steering.*[13]

These two hypotheses of the sociology of wisdom may in a general way be related to the two dominant literary types in instruction. One form, commonly called "instruction" by the scholars, is intentionally didactic.[14] It takes the form of imperative or prohibition (cf. Prov. 6:25–30). Such a way of instruction reflects a certain structure of authority. But much more frequent is the other form, the *saying,* which may be one line, a two-line parallel, or a fuller poem. This form explicitly claims no authority beyond the weight and persuasion of insight into the shape of the world.[15] There is no appeal here to external, extrinsic authority.[16] The saying intends to be genuinely empirical, growing out of a *tradition of experience,* but also making contact with the *experience of the listener.* Its authority depends on the appeal to good sense made by the statement itself.

It will be useful for church educators to reflect on these two hypotheses—*clan wisdom,* which helps people discern the shape, boundaries, and limits of conduct in the community and *court wisdom,* which addresses matters of power, freedom, and responsibility. Both yield important analogies for the teaching enterprise.[17] By way of a grounding hypothesis, we should also mention that a developed and likely derivative form of wisdom is mature, sophisticated theological reflection. We do not know about the setting for such an enterprise. Whybray has termed this the "intellectual tradition."[18] It appears to be a self-conscious tradition of quite insightful reflection on ethical and theological matters which is matched by delicate and artistic forms of literary expression. This tradition of teachers, scholars, and scientists had some kind of continuity, for it appears to be a learned art. At the same time, this tradition of reflection had some distance and freedom from conventional communal restraints. Followers of this tradition may have been the "eggheads" in the community who carried on the dangerous, extravagant, and imaginative probing of life. That perhaps represents yet another dimension of the wisdom tradition. Such an enterprise is not unrelated to the court hypothesis, but it suggests a "think tank" more removed from the teaching enterprise or the immediate intrigues of political action.

PATIENT OBSERVATION, EXPECTANT UNCERTAINTY

We begin, as we have in the other parts of the canon, with a question about the mode of knowledge. How does Israel know what it knows? It is clear that knowing here is very different from what we have found in the Torah and in the prophets. In the Torah, the question is asked, *"What do these stones mean?"* It is affirmed that the stones had a full, identifiable meaning which could be shared. There was a known agreement about the right answer. There was a consensus in the tradition, expressing a normative world-view, not at all in doubt. The prophetic canon asked, *"Is there any word from the Lord?"* The very question waits for and expects a new truth, which as often as not challenged the consensus over which the king presided. As we have seen, that new truth seems to have come from unlegitimated sources as a disruption of the consensus.

In this third part of the canon, with reference to wisdom, neither the way of the Torah nor the way of the prophets operates. We are not dealing with a *settled consensus* nor with a *radical break from the consensus*. We are rather in touch with a mystery that cannot be too closely shepherded, as in the Torah, or protested against, as in the prophets. There is here a not-knowing, a waiting to know, a patience about what is yet to be discerned, and a respect for not knowing that must be honored and not crowded. This way does not seek conclusions for immediate resolutions. It works at a different pace because it understands that the secrets cannot be forced.

The question on which we focus is from Job 28:12: *"Where shall wisdom be found?"* It is crucial that the question comes in this great chapter. Job 28 is placed at a decisive turn in the poetry. In the first twenty-seven chapters, Job and his friends argue around conventional presuppositions. But Job and friends up until this point assume that things can be known, and if necessary, forced. After Job 28, there is a pitiful protest by Job and then the great speeches of the whirlwind which shatter all the conventions. Job 28 provides the daring move from a *conventional quarrel* to a confrontation which *reduces all the conventions of a disputation to irrelevance.*[19]

As commonly held, it is likely that Job 28 is not created for this spot, but has been located in its present place secondarily. Although that may be so, we can deal with it only as it now stands. Job 28 asks the hard question about the source of wisdom. It knows that wisdom entails a great brooding. So the answer is not given easily or unambiguously. For this poem struggles with nothing less than that we do not finally know the source or placement of wisdom. Job 28 is marvelously located. On the one hand, *it looks back,* back to the first twenty-seven chapters of Job, back to the simplistic assumptions of Job 1–2 and the arguments of Job and friends which end in a lack of resolution. It also looks back to the tradition of Proverbs in which the teachers proceeded with some confidence. Looking back, 28:12 is answered: Wisdom is found in the experience of the world. The object which contains wisdom is the world, the created order. The appropriate way to knowledge is by engagement with the world. This requires fascination, imagination, patience, attentiveness to detail, and finally, observation of the regularities which seem to govern.[20] Wisdom is found in the experience of the specific, concrete experiences which individuals discern for themselves. But because the experienced world is ordered and orderly, constant, regular, and reliable, there is a *more generalized experience* of the community. What the keen observer sees in his/her experience is something that this community of observers has seen again and again, over a long period of time. There is a *tradition of experience* and an *immediacy of experience.* These together provide wisdom enough to relate to the world.

Such wisdom, because it is experiential, is not dogmatic. At its best, it tries to take account of all experience. It knows that new experience may cause a revision in the conclusions reached thus far and that it must be as clear as possible, given the present state of experience. But it is cautious and provisional about systematization. Thus it proceeds concretely. Clearly, after one has observed the same again and again, the concrete observation hardens into conviction. After a while, it is difficult to entertain the possibility of experience and observation which would resist the generalization. That is the crisis for Job and his friends. Both had learned for so long about the way life is ordered so that they are thrown into disarray by an experience which the generalization cannot contain.[21] The proper order of such knowledge is clear. First, there is *observation*, then *generalization*, and then *exploration* to see how, in what ways, and to what extent new experience fits the generalization and to what extent it challenges, disputes, or overthrows the generalization.

The mood of such instruction is dialogical at two levels. There is a dialogue between teacher and learner, between the ones with more experience and those with less, between the tradition of experience and the immediacy of experience.[22] But there is also the dialogue of all the learners (including the teacher) with the stuff of life. It is the stuff of life, that which is given to us in the world around us, which claims attention, which yields so much to the attentive observer, and yet which toughly withholds much that we want to know. So there is required of the learners both a forceful insistence that the world should yield its secrets and, at the same time, a patient respect for the truth which will not be forced.

That is where wisdom shall be found—in the stuff of life, the world, our experience. This tradition believes that the world is not neutral, not accidental, not passive. It holds for the patient, diligent observer what needs to be known. And what needs to be known are the shapes of regularity, reliability, recurring which permit control, prediction, and anticipation. Thus fascination with the ordered world is a form of creation faith and the rootage of scientific knowledge.[23]

Job 28 looks back to the conviction that there is practical evidence of how life holds together. But we must immediately correct that judgment. Such a judgment about the question of 28:12, taken by itself, claims too much. The chapter not only looks back in a conserving, conservative posture, but also *forward*[24] to the militant posture of Job in 29—31, where he defiantly storms heaven and gets nothing for it. It is Job's forward leaning that discovers that knowledge will not be forced, and that God withholds more than he discloses. Job 28 looks forward to the whirlwind of 38—41 in which it is clear that this massive sovereign need not respond to any human question and need not accommodate any categories which reduce knowledge to human capability.[25] Job 28 also looks forward to Ecclesiastes, which no longer has the buoyant confidence of Proverbs or the strident assurance of Job's friends, but only a recognition that wisdom is not available to human persons, either in experience or anywhere else:

> However much man may toil in seeking, he will not find it out; even though a wise man claims to know, he cannot find it out (Eccles. 8:17).

All wisdom is held by God alone. None other can know. That is, our best knowing involves a recognition of inscrutability that cannot be dispelled because the ultimate Knower as well as ultimate knowledge is withheld from us. That also must be taught in the faithful community. The matter must be held didactically. Job 28 is a pivot for that. Wisdom in Job 28 is *looking back to human confidence*. It is *looking forward to divine inscrutability*. That is the way of our experience. There is a knowing and there is an inability to know. So there is knowledge given in faithful experience and there is knowledge retained for God alone. The former of these is crucial against a kind of *abdicating obscurantism* which refuses to know or think or take responsibility. The latter of these is crucial against a kind of *shameless scientism* which knows no limits, which bows before no mystery, and which reduces all of life to a technique.

I submit that education in the faithful community might usefully explore this demanding dialectic. It is our task to nurture folks to take responsibility for what can be known. But it is equally our responsibility that mystery should not be regarded as ignorance.[26] That dialectic requires a special care for education. Education is nurturing people into the practice of discernment, of watching slowly, patiently, enduringly, to see what will be given us. This is the kind of watching which knows that our own experience must be held under critical scrutiny to find out about the gifts of the Creator. It is a much more demanding knowledge than that of the Torah. We have called knowledge in the Torah *disclosure*. In the twinkling of the eye, something was shown to Israel that was immediately known to be true. But here we cannot speak simply of disclosure because there is as much hidden as there is given. In the same way we cannot speak, as with the prophets, of *disruption*, for this is not forced or explosive. It is not a break which charges against us, as does the prophetic world. It is more like a gradual dawning, a slow coming together of insights, a recognition which comes at its own pace, so that we do not recall when we learned it.

So we have here neither *disclosure* nor *disruption*, but *discernment*. The educational task, then, is to discern and to teach to discern, to attend to the gifts given in experience, to attend to the world around us. It is to read ourselves and that world in its playfulness, to know that what immediately meets the eye is not all there is. It is to know that as we touch the dailyness of our lives, we are in touch also with something precious beyond us that draws close to the holiness of God. In this way we learn that in our knowing we have not been permitted to know fully, but only in a mirror darkly (1 Cor. 13:12).

The dialectic of Job 28, which looks *back to confident experience* and *forward to inscrutability*, is perhaps best stated in the formula of Job 1:21 "The Lord gave, and the Lord has taken away." At one level that sounds uncritically pious. But if we linger there, it may suggest something else. It may suggest that as the Lord gives, we are free to probe fully and exult in our knowledge. But the Lord also takes away. This may mean that the truth is always out beyond, and we are left only to revere and to wait. Our calling is not to choose one of these over the other, not to prefer either the giving or the taking away, not to relish exclusively in the knowledge from experience or the knowledge held to God alone. Rather, true discernment or genuine wisdom is to stay with God in the seasons, to move in and out on the giving which lets us understand, and on to the taking away which places us always in new perspective. That dialectic has been hopelessly collapsed in much of our education. Both belong. Both are crucial for mature faith, and which of the two is to be emphasized depends very much on where people are and how the world is understood. Von Rad comments:

> Obviously Israel, in her 'enlightened' understanding of the world, has stumbled upon a dialectic of experience which could no longer be simply resolved and released. Indeed, if Yahweh and the world had been identical, then everything could have been expressed in simple

terms. But Yahweh encountered man in the world always and only in the individual act of experience, and this certainly did not presuppose any identity of God and world. Again, the expressions 'experiences of Yahweh' and 'experience of the world' perhaps did not entirely coincide . . . the teachers were completely unaware of any reality not controlled by Yahweh.[27]

It is moving back and forth in this dialectic that concerns this way of knowledge.

In light of that general characterization of the mode of knowledge, we may consider briefly some of the forms in which this knowledge was practiced.[28]

1. As indicated, one major form is instruction, which is directly didactic. As we have seen, von Rad does not regard it as a central representative form of wisdom teaching, perhaps because it is too heavy and not playful enough. We may take as a foremost example Prov. 3:7, which was already cited by Gerstenberger as typical and a fair summary of clan wisdom.

This teaching includes one prohibition and two imperatives. The prohibition protests against the notion that the person is a possessor of knowledge (cf. Isa. 10:12–14). The positives together assert the transcendence of God ("fear the Lord") and moral possibility for the one addressed. The linkage of *transcendence* and *morality* is shown to be precarious and provisional by the negative warning about pride and the assumption of knowing too much. Thus the terse statement presents an entire life-world. At the same time, the intent of the teacher is left quite open and yet is stated concretely. The wise person is to "shun evil," but so little is identified. What is evil? How does one know it, and how does one avoid it? Likely the saying established a frame for interaction which remains to be filled out by experience. Thus, at one and the same time, the epistemology offers a *clear structure for knowledge,* but the *substance remains to be decided on the basis of pragmatic and experiential grounds.* Evil is what diminishes life and disrupts community. It is not known in advance what that might be. While such instruction is not lacking in authority, it is easy to imagine the teacher setting case studies or inviting students to contribute from their own experience and observation about what enhances and disrupts life. The saying, however, does not permit a singular focus on morality because the large question of "fear of Yahweh" still remains. Thus the saying holds together world-experience and Yahweh-experience.

2. A second form of teaching is the numerical saying (cf. Prov. 6:16–19; 30:18–19, 21–23, 24–28, 29–31). These texts invite the listener to classify and enumerate things so that common ingredients become obvious.

Six things Yahweh hates (6:16–19),

Four things that are inscrutable (30:18–19),

Four things which cause the earth to tremble (30:21–23),

Four things that are very small and very wise (30:24–28),

Four things proud and stately (30:29–31).

The teaching surely appeals to good learning theory. It moves from things known, but it invites imagination that requires a new configuration of data. The mode is open-ended and admits of alternative answers. What should not be missed is a playfulness in articulation. The list has become stable, but it by no means precludes further reflection and probing. The articulation is aware of the *inscrutability* of our best knowing which is kept open for revision. It invites *imagination*, for it presents pictures of a strutting cock, a strutting king, or a man in love. The teaching at the same time enjoys the *particularity* of the concrete example, and yet forms a network of scientific data by grouping things together. The shrewdness of the saying is a focus on both the *commonalities* and the *distinctive* qualities. I suggest that the value of such a form is not only for its own substance, but for the model of other knowledge. If one is working with young people, for example, the model might evoke: Name four things which cause fear in high school persons; name seven things about which national leaders regularly lie. The list goes on and on, and in the process two things happen: (1) our powers of discernment are teased and opened, and (2) we become aware of the givenness of life which amuses and abides. This is indeed scientific learning, for it seeks for categories and genres. But it is scientific learning that requires discernment, arrangement, and flexibility.

3. A third and much-used form is the *two-line saying* which tries to

locate the boundary between acceptable and unacceptable conduct.
Notice how practical this knowledge is. It does not ask about what is,
but about what one does. The two-line saying might be likened to a
multiple choice question, only there are two differences. First, the
options presented require decision and never permit detachment.
Second, there is no chance to check "none of the above." The sayings
address quite concrete practical problems. But there is a seriousness,
because life hinges on them. So which will it be?

> He who tills his land will have plenty of bread,
>> but he who follows worthless pursuits has no sense (Prov. 12:11).
> A gift in secret averts anger;
>> and a bribe in the bosom, strong wrath (21:14).
> A soft answer turns away wrath,
>> but a harsh word stirs up anger (15:1).

In brief form, these three sayings lay out central questions for life.
The first asks about *work and leisure*. The second explores ways of
manipulating or managing *people* positively. The third focuses on the
possibilities of *speech*. The first and third state alternatives, and the
second gives two examples of one kind of gesture. Again, teaching is
concrete. But life is open. The world is fluid. The teacher and the
student are engaged in sorting out what is *given* and what is an *option*.
What appears to work on one day may not be the choice on another
day. The wisdom teachers know that the line between acceptable and
unacceptable behavior is very thin and hard to see. No hard judgments are made. But there is a firmness to life. There is a sure sense
of cause and effect, a premise that there are predictable links between
acts and consequences.[29] The aim is that persons should reflect on
behavior and be attentive to the possibilities for life that come with
certain kinds of conduct.

4. A variation on the two-line form is the "better saying."[30] We
might call this "prioritizing objectives." Some things are preferable
to others. But perhaps they are preferable only in certain circumstances. You know the game. If you are on an ocean cruise, rank in
order the things you must take along. So some things are preferable
to others:

Herbs are better than a fatted ox . . . (under certain circumstances)
(Prov. 15:17).
A good name is better than riches (22:1). Would this have been said by
a poor person or someone already secure?
To be poor is better than to be perverse (Prov. 28:6).

The same style is used for things religious: Torah is sweeter than gold
(Ps. 19:10, cf. Eccles. 7:3,5). Such a way of thinking gives marvelous
teaching opportunities for something like "values clarification."
Only these sayings do not simply ask people which they prefer. They
use the value terms, "good/better." They permit and require one to
go on to ask: How better? In what way and by what norms? How
does one decide what is better? It is clear that the wisdom teachers
who speak this way have a clearly ordered sense of values. They do
not believe that all of this is yet to be decided. The sayings enunciate
and presume an entire world view. But the sayings which are not at
all neutral conceal as much as they disclose. In the process, they force
the learner to the most fundamental questions.

5. A much-used form among the wisdom teachers is the metaphor
and simile. They observe that something is like something else:

A poor man who oppresses the poor
   is a beating rain that leaves no food (Prov. 28:3).
Like a roaring lion or a charging bear
   is a wicked ruler over a poor people (28:15).
Like snow in summer or rain in harvest,
   so honor is not fitting for a fool (26:1).

In 26:7–18, there is a barrage of such figures; a lame man's legs; one
who binds stone in a sling; a thorn that goes into the hand of a
drunkard; an archer who wounds everybody; a dog that returns to his
vomit; a person who takes a passing dog by the ear; a madman who
throws firebrands, arrows, and death. The figures are vivid and concrete. They rush past and require hard work. They teach conduct
and values by making surprising comparisons and linkages. But they
do not tell too much. One is still left with the question: in what way is
it like? In what way is it unlike? The wisdom teachers seek for commonalities and patterns and comparisons. But much is left for the

learner. I have the impression that much church education has not been respectful enough about the mystery of knowledge and has told too much. The way of metaphor invites listeners to think anew, to see afresh, to discern differently. Each time this way is used, something is concealed. One becomes aware of how much is not given or known (cf. 1 Cor. 13:12).

The list could be continued, but the main tendencies are clear. The major form yet to be observed is what von Rad describes as "the long didactic poem."[31] This is more of an artistic treatise. It utilizes various skills and devices of wisdom instruction. It is a probing against and a struggling with a world that does not easily surrender. It lives at the point where new hunch and old conviction intersect. And the battle is to force a new insight.

Of all of these and the other forms that might be catalogued, the main points to be observed are:

1. The teaching focuses on experience. The stuff of teaching comes out of daily life.

2. Daily life is not handled in a vacuum; it is understood as having a shape which must be respected and honored, but also carefully discerned.

3. The mode is dialogic in structure. The teaching is evocative. Both parties are engaged. New understandings are possible as both parties engage in thoughtful discernment.

4. There is a playfulness and delight that goes with it. The play involves not only good humor, but the "play" about which we speak in a steering wheel. There is slippage that cannot be overcome or explained. To want more certainty is to crush the wonder that belongs to knowing.

5. The teaching, unlike that of Torah and prophets, is just for today. That is, it has a provisional quality which leaves things open for another experience. The claim is modest. Sufficient for the day is the mystery thereof (cf. Matt. 6:34).

This kind of teaching is hard work. It requires a great deal of work on the spot. It demands imaginative "ad hocishness." But that imagination works in a field of orderly conviction. Experience is seen by the teacher not as a disordered mass, but as a sensible configuration. The task of instruction is to teach the new ones to see in the midst of the disorder a coherence that can be relied on. Teaching may be giving people eyes to see.

HOLY INTERCONNECTEDNESS

Now we turn to our second question, to ask about the *substance* of wisdom teaching. What did the wisdom teachers know? What did they think important to transmit? They are not sophists who engage in a merely formal process, but they are clearly believers of a convinced kind.

1. These teachers affirm that the construction and maintenance of human community is a human task. It is dangerous and difficult and always uncertain. Although there is no one else to do it, it can be done. For good reason, scholars have seen that this is Israel's best "humanism."[32] The wisdom teachers offer a celebration of human freedom and human responsibility and, in the case of Job, human *hutzpah.* This instruction is perhaps reflected in Psalm 8[33] on the one hand, and Deut. 30:11–14 on the other. It is affirmed that "you can do it," and you are authorized to do it. Moreover, you must do it and continue to do it because the task persists. While such a charter for human imagination and human initiative may be implicit in the other literature, here it is the agenda. The wisdom teachers bring people to a profoundly human world in which the real questions take anthropocentric form.[34]

2. The doing that human persons must do is premised on *good knowing.* Knowing is a good thing. What needs to be known for life can be found out, and it is a good thing to find out. Finding out belongs to the human enterprise. There is no stress here on revelation, and even the revelation of the whirlwind to Job is not so much a disclosure as it is a concealment. The shift is *from revelation to discovery.* Knowing now becomes a human enterprise. The primary agent in the knowing process is shifted to a human agenda. The human person is not only the passive recipient of knowledge, but the generator of new knowledge not known before. There are, of

course, risks in such knowing. It may be, as Mendenhall[35] suggests, that Genesis 2—3 is the dark side of knowledge. And Gen. 11:1–9 warns against knowing so that nothing is impossible. Things are given over into human hands.

3. But the matter must be stated dialectically. The wisdom urged on Israel is not technical information. We are not dealing with a kind of positivism in which everything can be known. This knowledge only drives one deeper into the mystery. So even this humanistic education is finally theonomous. That is, it has to do with God.[36] At the bottom of our knowing is a mystery, which is God's rule. That mystery is as dangerous as evil, as holy as God, and as demanding as morals. Thus what Israel here knows is *dangerous* knowledge, *transcendent* knowledge, *demanding* knowledge.

The mystery belongs to God, who has not turned it over to any human person—not to the king or the scientist or the theologian (Gen. 40:8).

The mystery is generous and well-inclined toward humankind. Or to say it another way, the Creator values the creation. God wills good for his creatures, but "good" must be on his terms. Wisdom is discerning those terms which are not subject to accommodation or bargaining. The mystery is to be discerned. But that is not equivalent to solving a problem.

The mystery of God is not a general good feeling. It is a *plan.*[37] The world is created for a purpose. That purpose will work its way. Human persons can be a part of that purpose. They can, at most, delay the plan. But they cannot resist it (Gen. 50:20). That is, wisdom finally drives Israel toward the resilient, even if hidden, sovereignty of God. While the experiences of the world may be presented in many different ways, all of them attest to the one who governs this life-giving process in his own inscrutable pleasure.

We are thus pressed into the arena of providence *(provideo)*. God sees ahead and supplies the need of the creation (Ps. 145:15–16). Von Rad has identified those proverbial sayings that put human conduct into the persistent framework of divine purpose (Prov. 16:2, 9, 33; 19:21; 20:24; 21:2; 21:30, 31).[38] Providence of course is a difficult affirmation for us, becuase it inevitably requires us to face the question of predestination. The wisdom teachers of Israel did not press that far.[39] Even in the late, most cynical statements, they stop short of the full logic of predestination.[40] They are content to say that it is God's world, and all our claims for human knowledge, human freedom, and human responsibility must be set in that context. The deep riddle of wisdom is the full affirmation of human responsibility and the full affirmation of God's sovereign purpose. And these teachers do not choose between them.[41]

The mystery of God's ultimate rule is a reality both of *limits* and of *gift*. There are limits beyond which persons cannot go without destruction.[42] There is a gift at the center, the remarkable gift of perseverance, sustenance, and nourishment which is miraculously given to us. The *gift* taken alone may lead to careless exploitation or, as in the case of Job, to imagining that things will be settled on human terms.[43] But the *limit*, taken alone as in the case of Job's friends, can lead to pettiness and bitterness. Education out of these traditions requires us to be quite dialectical, to enjoy the full celebration of human ingenuity and human capacity for world building, and, at the same time and in the same breath, the affirmation of God's mystery which issues in doxology, amazement, and gratitude.

The wisdom teachers affirm that human experience bespeaks God's gracious mystery. It is the juxtaposition of these themes that matters:

> It is the glory of God to conceal things,
>> but the glory of kings is to search things out.
> As the heavens for height, and the earth for depth,
>> so the mind of kings is unsearchable (Prov. 25:2–3).[44]

Both God and humankind have their proper work. The drama of concealing and searching out is the main vocation of human persons. Human persons are recalled to *power*. Much power comes in knowledge. This knowledge, however, leads not only to power. It may also lead to *praise*. And it is *praise* that conceals and redefines power. Thus the upshot of wisdom teaching is not *techniques* for management, but it is finally *doxology* which is based on wonder, awe, and amazement.·

4. However, the dialectic must be corrected again. We must not turn it too far toward the experience of God. In the midst of doxology toward God, there is still the experience of the world that claims our best attention. What do we discern if we study the world? Most of all we learn of its orderliness and reliability, its continuity and regularity. Von Rad has shown that even the most innocent looking proverb is not just casual chatter.[45] Rather, each such proverb is an enduring summary of long-tested experience. Events are not observed one at a time. Each proverb is a "system analysis." Specific observations are pressed to generalization. The wisdom teachers are concerned with the *kinds* of consequences that regularly flow from certain *kinds* of action.

Both the premise and the conclusion of such study and analysis are the judgment that *life is connected.* The connection is attested by daily experience and is wrought by the abiding rule of God. I submit that it is the discovery, premise, assumption, and conviction of the *interconnectedness of life* that is the central substance of the wisdom teachers.[46] The interconnectedness of life is an enormous problem. On the one hand, obscurantists, superstitious people, and naive children imagine connections that do not exist. But how does one know when a linkage is correct or is an imagination? Medical science, for example, is based on the connections of medicines and bodily responses. Attention to the strange phenomena of *placebo,* however, gives us pause and reminds us that the interconnections are much more concealed than we like to think.[47]

Still, it is the opposite danger that is more prevalent for us. The danger among us is not to imagine that life is too much connected. Rather, the danger is to assume that on the basis of technical competence, life is not connected, or we can outflank the connections, or we have some options about the nature of the connections if we are wise and strong enough.

Berger has shown that the bureaucratic consciousness is based on the notion that life is not connected.[48] Life is made up of components which have no necessary linkage to one another. Therefore life can be parceled out in administrative units and dealt with a piece at a time. So we can separate private and public goals, social action and evangelism, foreign policy and racial justice.[49]

We learn so late and so often in public life that our power does not give us the capacity to connect life differently. There are certain *givens,* ordained of God, that no administrator can overcome. Thus, for example, the disaster of governments who seek to separate tribes from land, to give people security instead of freedom, to replace families with bureaus, to replace religion with ideology. It is often thought that life can be discerned rationally; that given careful reasoning, there is no part of life that cannot be administered differently. Such a rationality, of course, means to veto the mystery and reshape life in our own image.

Now, the problem of course is that we don't know and cannot know. Perhaps there may be some discoveries or revolutions that will show the current presuppositions about connections to be null and void. Perhaps what we have taken to be ordained of God is nothing more than a social habit or convention. Maybe some revision is possible on any given point. So an effort must be made.

To such a large "perhaps," wisdom teachers would have made two responses. First, we have to deal with the data at hand and not speculate beyond it. These teachers are relentlessly experiential. We have to take life as it comes and see where things yield or where they do not yield. Second, new data will not lead to a conclusion that life is disconnected. That is a bottom line for the teachers.[50] Rather, it will lead to new depths of interconnectedness. The World is one and God is Lord of it all. We do not yet have the last data; so we have much to explore. All the exploration moves toward a sense of coherence. Thus the wisdom teachers are on their way (never arrived, but on the way) to discerning the rationality, the *logos,* the enduring ordering of reality which is God-given and which endures in the face of every assault and every discontinuity. The teachers dared to believe that this *logos* can be discerned in *daily experience,* if we are attentive. On the other hand, they held that ordering will not be bypassed or overcome by

our daily decisions. It abides and endures. Our human work is to discern always more fully how that mysterious linkage is shaped.

Education in this tradition pays close attention to the data. It also
has this overriding conviction that lies under the data. One is always
trying to read between the lines. That is why wisdom must be playful, exploratory, and tentative. The wisdom teachers do not doubt for
a moment that life is interconnected. Even in Ecclesiastes, when the
preacher decides that the data will not yield clues to us, he does not
doubt the linkage. Modern folk may abandon the conviction in their
practice of technical reason. But these wisdom teachers finally abandoned the *data* in order to hold to the *connection.*[51] The conviction
was kept in place for another time when others would return to the
data and see again how that conviction was evidenced in daily life.

Thus the wisdom teachers do not draw conclusions, except as in
the case of Job's friends. Mostly they explore problems and offer
hints. They are for the most part not interested in speculative questions, but only in questions that concern human conduct and human
hope. That is, the issue is always *ethics* and not *metaphysics.* In Proverbs, the ethical question concerns humankind. In Job, it is the ethics
of God. In Ecclesiastes the question is turned from God in agnosti-
cism, and there is a new emphasis on human ethics. At its best, the
counsel of the wise believes that in our world, deeds have predictable
consequences. There are no deeds without consequences. We live in a
morally coherent universe in which our actions create "spheres of
destiny" which we cannot resist.[52] The world as God has ordered it
will not be mocked.

Now, I submit that this opens an important educational enterprise.
It insists that education should be centrally ethical. It insists that
ethics is focused on the providential ordering of life with God. As a
result, life and our choices are inescapable. Except for Job's destruc-
tive friends, however, the ethical teaching of wisdom is not heavy-
handed, not doctrinaire, not knowing too much. It is teaching not
"from above," but "from below." By the time of Ecclesiastes, the
result may be cynically obedient persons. But the aim of the Book of
Proverbs is a morally sensitive person who is prepared to live responsibly in God's world.

It will be evident by this time that we have come nearly full circle to the Torah claim of obedience. But not quite. What separates the wisdom teachers from the certitude of Torah is their provisional quality. The wisdom teacher is neither a pliable heir who agrees to everything, as Murphy has shown, nor is he a rebellious cynic who rejects everything. Rather, the wisdom teacher is a faithful product of the tradition, for it is the fulness of the wisdom tradition not just to repeat and trust and parrot old judgments, but to make new judgments on the basis of new data. That is what this third epistemology hopes for. Not everything is up for grabs. The sure sovereign rule of God and the resultant interconnectedness of life are not negotiable. In that context, what is hoped for are morally alive people who keep the old answers under review and make new articulations of how life is being experienced. To the advocates of fixed Torah, such an enterprise is, of course, daring. But conversely, to those alive in the wisdom tradition, to hold to old Torah may be to deny new experience.[53] The wisdom teachers have sure confidence that rightly understood, new experience will not subvert old Torah but will enhance it and give it vitality for fresh coping. It is a risk. But risk-taking is mandatory in this tradition. Among the wisdom teachers, it is only a minority report (Job's friends) who want to freeze wisdom at some point. The main claim and identity of the tradition is that the world must be recharacterized and reunderstood and rearticulated as long as God's people have new experiences.

So we come back to the poem of Job 28.[54] In the beginning, (vv. 1–11) we are told about human capacity and human probing. If the secret of life were of the earth, human persons would know it, for they can mine and move mountains, cut out channels, recover precious stones, control water, "unearth" everything. And that is useful. But for the present question, it is of no avail. The question remains: "Where is wisdom to be found?" (v. 12).

Then in vv. 13–22, we have a negative recital of *where wisdom is not:*

It is not in the earth. Human persons cannot find it (v. 13).

It is not in the sea (v. 14).

It is not in gold and silver (v. 15).

It is not in precious minerals (vv. 16–19).

In the book of Job, until this chapter, both Job and his friends thought they had access, even control. But clearly all that is now superseded.

The distinction between God and humankind remains. Our best learning is limited. There is no way to possess the mystery of life. It is hidden (v. 21).[55] Reflection on experience is worthwhile, but it is limited. It should not be pressed beyond its limit.

Then, in vv. 23–27, God is distanced from the human enterprise. "Only God!" God knows. God is the Lord of wisdom. He searches it out. But humankind will not. Wisdom is not entrusted to humankind and will not be grasped. We have seen earlier how the Book of Proverbs worked with the same distancing, especially in the texts of 16:2, 9; 19:21; 20:24; 21:2, 30–31. The wisdom teachers worked continually with the dialectic of world-experience and Yahweh-experience. The two forms of experience converge. They are held together in the same sayings. But they are never identified. Now, after Proverbs and in Job 28, there is distancing. Clearly Job and his friends have drawn too close. They had made an easy equation between their moral commitments and the ways of Yahweh. They knew too much, and so they presumed on God. So in this poem, there is a distancing. Like Job and Job's friends, Job 28 does not doubt that there is a wisdom in the world, an order. But it is not fully knowable. All our discernments of it are proximate and provisional. We are at the edge of *logos* theology. The rationality of the world is discernible in hints, but not manageable in totality. There is an order, a coherence, a regularity. But it is not contained in human rationality. Before the rationality of God, there can only be reverence and praise. For all the confident probing of Proverbs, we still must come to this conclusion. Proverbs suggests many helpful pedagogical points of entry. We have mentioned values clarification, prioritizing objectives, multiple choice, locating boundaries, and tension with old tradition. All of these are worth pursuing. But the end of wisdom does not lie there. Rather, it lies in awe before the throne of God. *Discernment* of life culminates in *praise*. Education consists finally in teaching our young to sing doxologies.

So the text battles with what this conviction means for the life of Israel. Proverbs has become too confident, too flatly ethical. But the main thrust of Job 28, if left alone, is too remotely theological. So in vv. 27–28, there is a neat juxtaposition of themes, surely reminiscent of Prov. 25:2–3. On the one hand, in v. 27, God is Lord of wisdom:

> Then he saw it and declared it;
> he established it, and searched it out.

On the other hand, in v. 28, human persons trust God's wisdom by obeying:

> Behold, the fear of the Lord, that is wisdom.
> And to depart from evil is understanding.

These two verses say it well. There is an awesome acknowledgment of God, and there is a sober recognition of humankind. The two have to do with each other. But they have to do with each other at a distance. We are left with a terribly modest conclusion, befitting the role of human persons in the creation of God. The best human *knowing* takes the form of *discerning obedience*.

It has been suggested that v. 28 is an addition, a toning down of the grand and negative statement. While that is possible, I am not convinced of it.[56] Rather it is the necessary follow-up on that statement. So in v. 28, we come full circle to Prov. 3:7.[57] Wisdom is to fear God, to let God be God, to let mystery be definitional for life. Understanding is to depart from evil, that is, to stay at the concrete, daily task of human community with all its ethical risks.

Such a sober conclusion drawn from such an eloquent probe reminds me of a tale I have heard third-hand and cannot verify. Henry Nouwen made a journey to India to explore with Mother Teresa the clue to faithful living. If anyone would know, it was she. Faced with such a profound question, her answer shocks with simplicity: "Spend an hour with God each day and don't do anything you know is wrong." That simple, authoritative response sounds like the come-down of v. 28. Wisdom is not so hidden that we cannot act wisely day after day. The end of wisdom is very close to its beginning. It begins in the "fear of the Lord" (Prov. 1:7). Its end is the fear of the Lord (Job 28: 28).[58] This fear becomes a bracket for our daily life in which we live responsibly with the daily riddle, the daily freedom, and the daily burden.

Our question is posed in v. 12: "Where shall wisdom be found?" Our answer is not a simple one. The main argument of the poem is that wisdom is found with God and is not accessible to humankind. But v. 28 adds an important hint. Not all of wisdom is available to humankind, but some of it is. And that is enough for nurture, for faith, and for life.

5
Obedience as a Mode of Knowledge

We have considered three elements of Israel's scripture under the guidance of Jer. 18:18. We have suggested that in each of these elements there is to be found both a *mode* of knowledge and a *substance* that should concern us in our educational task:

1. The *ethos* of our community knows that the memory of the stones is given, settled, and can be trusted. We embrace the *consensus of the Torah.* We have a *disclosure* of God's purpose for and way with his people. That disclosure is sure and undoubted among us.

2. The *pathos* of God leads to a giving of *new truth in uncredentialed channels.* The consensus is shattered by the *disruptive word of the prophet.* In this poetry of *pathos,* the royal definitions of reality are overcome, to end what cannot be ended, to begin what cannot be begun.

3. The *logos* of God is the sure ordering of created reality. It is an ordering which requires *wisdom to discern*—an ordering which leads to responsibility and freedom, but also to mystery and awe. The order of life is at times available to us and at times hidden from us. Wisdom is the readiness both to penetrate the mystery and to live obediently with its inscrutability.

It should be clear that as these elements constitute different pieces of literature, so they also present different intellectual, theological, and educational perspectives. Hopefully it is equally clear that we are not free to choose one of these to the neglect of the others. The juxtaposition of *ethos* which assures, *pathos* which wrenches, and *logos* which instructs, is crucial. The practice of *disclosure, disruption,* and *discernment* all are important in faithful living. The life of faith consists in treasuring the consensus, breaking the consensus with new truth, and valuing new experience in tension with the tradition of experience.

"THOU" IN THE PSALMS

But we have unfinished business. We have considered the facets outlined in Jer. 18:18. Yet no treatment of our subject is complete without some attention to the Psalms. The Psalms, of course, are not referred to in the summary of Jer. 18:18. Nevertheless, they are undoubtedly a dominant element in the third part of the canon, the writings, and must be reckoned along with Torah and prophets as a major resource for faith. Thus in adding this consideration to our discussion, we must break out of the tripartite division of Jer. 18:18. If it is important to stay with the canonical divisions, then we must simply say that the third division in the canon requires us to deal with both Psalms and wisdom. In any case, we shall consider here what we can learn in particular from the Psalms in relation to the educational process.

There is a problem in trying to make any comprehensive claim for the Psalms by way of generalization. On the one hand, the *particularity* of the Psalms makes it necessary to comment on each individual poem, a task clearly beyond us here. On the other hand, we must forego a *reduction,* as though this powerful and diverse material could be caught in such a way.

Our comments here presume a general scholarly consensus concerning the form and life-setting of the Psalms. Scholarship has found it exceedingly difficult to move beyond the positions of Gunkel and Mowinckel.[1] It is likely that Westermann's summary in terms of *Klage und Loben,* lament and praise, can serve us well, though that admittedly does not encompass all the Psalms.[2]

My purpose here is to make only one point about the Psalms. Then I shall hope to show how crucial that one point is for our educational task. The Psalms are the stylized, direct speech of Israel addressed to God.[3] The fact that this speech is *stylized* means that it does not have all the immediacy of raw religious confrontation. The style serves to preserve the speech from generation to generation. It also democratizes it so that ordinary people may speak it as well as a daring spiritual elite. It should give us pause that this simple traditional speech is still the best way we have to speak to God about all sorts and conditions of humankind. No amount of inventiveness has been able to improve upon this tradition.

That it is stylized does not detract from its *directness*. This is a speech that is not contaminated by technical theological reflection. It also is not screened through the language of piety or mysticism or contemplation. It is the kind of speech possible between two parties who are on terms clear enough and sound enough to risk and to offer candor. That is, it is covenantal speech that understands the exchange to be one between centers of power.[4] Because language is so crucial to human community, education in the church can be understood as nurture in language, of learning how we speak in this community, what we say, and to whom it may be said. Because language is evocative as well as descriptive,[5] language is crucial in nurturing people to a good confession. The premise and claim of the Psalms is that Israel has access to God. That is a given in this relationship. We shall comment later on the nearness of God as a theme of this tradition. But the practice of that *access* and the mode of that *nearness* are most important. The theme of nearness is important because it becomes a paradigm for other social relationships.[6] How God is loved is decisive for how the neighbor is loved. But it is also important in itself, for our speech with God determines *how* we know and *what* we know. Therefore education must take time and energy for speech with God.

1. The speech of the Psalms, corporate and personal, is a direct address to a "Thou."[7] The church has to learn again in every generation that we have to do with a specific, identifiable known "Thou," with whom we have a past and from whom we are promised a future. The utterance of this "Thou" gathers together that whole past. The Psalter is not engagement with a stranger, but with a long-standing

companion.[8] The utterance of this "Thou" amounts to a recital of the whole history of cost and suffering, joy and grief. This is clear in the intentional historical recitals as in Psalms 78, 105, 106, 136. But it is also the case in the lament Psalms which recount pasts of mutual fidelity, as in 22:4–5; 77:11–20. The nurture of "Thou-speech" is a guard on two fronts, both of which have urgency in the church. On the one hand, the "Thou" of the Psalms is a guard against *generalized religion* which is an unspecified feeling, a generalized hope, or a romantic good intention. The "Thou" of the Psalms has specificity. It is the Lord of Israel, the Maker of heaven and earth, and finally the Father of our Lord Jesus Christ. The Psalms have to be used very selectively and irresponsibly for this to be generalized religious poetry. For there is a scandalous Jewishness about these words.[9] To use them is to stand in this particular tradition.[10]

The second front which the "Thou" guards is a pervasive *narcissism* which is endlessly fascinated with ourselves, which regards ourselves as the ultimate reference. Karl Barth has made persistent case that the great modern problem and the heritage of the enlightenment is *autonomy*, the notion of self-grounding.[11] The "Thou" of the Psalms is a firm counter-affirmation against self-grounding. The Psalms assert that we are grounded in another and that we take our life from another. This may be the most urgent educational task facing the church—to enable persons to accept life and vocation as being grounded in another whose name and purpose we know.[12]

The "Thou" to whom Israel speaks, of course, is not derivative from "I" or "we," but is the promise of I and we. So Buber's classic articulation of "I-Thou" did not come out of a special mystical tradition, but out of the main tendency of the Old Testament.[13] The one whom we know as "Thou" is the one who has moved first, who has been responsive to us, who has "heard our cry and seen our affliction and come down to us and delivered us" (Exod. 3:7–8). Our address to this "Thou" is never the first form of address. It is always our answer, always a response, always a saying yes to a "YES" already said over us (cf. 2 Cor. 1:19).

The actual linguistic problem of saying yes is of two kinds. First, to say "Thou" requires a deep and concrete faith in God. One cannot speak a "Thou" into an empty sky. Second, if one is fixed on the self, the utterance of "Thou" is a dangerous diminishment, a violation of my self as ultimate concern. This "Thou" is not addressed easily or carelessly or off-handedly; such an address in fact amounts to a *reorientation of one's life*.

Many examples of this might be cited. One of the clearest is in Psalm 77.[14] In vv. 1–10 we have a lament which refers to God only in the third person. It is saturated with first person pronouns. The speaker retains initiative. Then, in vv. 11–12, the speaker begins to turn away from the "I" dominated present to the past filled with God's wonders. Finally, in v. 14, God is addressed as "Thou." In the transitional verses, 11–13, there is an approach by "your wonders, your work, your mighty deeds, your way." But like a massive turn, the "Thou" of v. 14 is decisive. Following that "Thou" is a review of the saving past. There is no more use of "I"; now it is all "thy" and "thou," with the conclusion in v. 20, "Thou didst lead thy people." There is a contentment to leave it with "Thou." The structure of the Psalm is instructive:

vv. 1–10   I——the present
vv. 11–20   Thou——the past

The past is utilized as an alternative way to enter the present. It cannot be concluded that the Psalm is an escape to the past, but rather it permits a revision of the present. The present is now understood as an arena dominated by the same "Thou." This does not mean that it is all sweetness and light. It means that when the "Thou" is crowded out, the "I" predictably lacks the resources to cope.

The point is made frequently and nearly at random in the Psalms. The "Thou" of Yahweh is a court of appeal against every form of helplessness and hopelessness. The "Thou" can be uttered when the "I" is exhausted and without resource. It is the "Thou" that inverts the circumstance:

But Thou, O Lord, art a shield about me,
my glory, and the lifter of my head (3:3).

For *Thou* art not a God who delights in wickedness;
  evil may not sojourn with thee . . .
For *thou* dost bless the righteous, O Lord;
  thou dost cover him with favor as with a shield (5:4, 12).
For *thou* hast maintained my just cause;
  thou hast sat on the throne giving righteous judgment.
Thou hast rebuked the nations,
Thou hast destroyed the wicked;
Thou hast blotted out their name for ever and ever (9:4–5).

Perhaps the best known of such turns is in Psalm 73.[15] The Psalm is easily divided into two parts. The first is a desperate, hopeless answer when the "I" tries to compete with the more successful autonomous agents. Then the Psalm takes an abrupt turn in v. 17. From this point on, life is reoriented, for it is filled with "Thou":

Truly *thou* dost set them in slippery places;
  thou dost make them fall to ruin . . .
Nevertheless I am continually with *thee;*
  thou dost hold my right hand.
Thou dost guide me with thy counsel,
  and afterward *thou* wilt receive me to glory . . .
thou dost put an end to those who are false to *thee* (vv. 18, 23–24, 27).

The utterance of a "Thou" is both a profound theological act and a bold, concrete linguistic act. It is profound theologically because it is a confessional statement, taking of sides, an affirmation about the shape of reality. It must also be a concrete linguistic act, not a thought, not a feeling, but a verbal, audible gesture which reorganizes one's life. Of course such a reading of reality flies in the face of much therapeutic opinion which encourages preoccupation with self. But finally, the crisis of life is this decision: either self-groundedness which becomes always more anguished, or liberated speech to the "Thou" who makes all things new.[16]

Martin Buber has preserved for us a song from the rabbi of Berditchev:[17]

Where I wander—You!
Where I ponder—You!

Only You, You again, always You!
You! You! You!
When I am gladdened—You!

When I am saddened—You!
Only You, You again, always You!
You! You! You!

Sky is You! Earth is You!

You above! You below!

In every trend, at every end,

Only You, You again, always You!

You! You! You!

The song echoes the irritation of the Psalmist:

If I ascend to heaven, thou art there!
    If I make my bed in Sheol, thou art there!
If I take the wings of the morning
    and dwell in the uttermost parts of the sea,
even there thy hand shall lead me,
    and thy right hand shall hold me.
If I say, "Let only darkness cover me,
    and the light about me be night,"
even the darkness is not dark to thee,
    the night is bright as the day;
    for darkness is as light with thee (Ps. 139:8–12).

The capacity to say "Thou" does not mean it is always a delight, but that in delight or in disaster, there is someone to address. Westerhoff has put the question, "Will Our Children have Faith?"[18] The answer to that is, "Of course." But what kind of faith? The Psalms wish for our children and for their parents this kind of directness which lives always toward the "Thou" whose name we know and whose history we share.

2. Now, of course, "Thou" can be a difficulty, depending on the substance of the "Thou." The models of Thou-ness we may have, may be mean, petty, coercive, oppressive, manipulative. But the Bible, specifically the Psalms, offers another "Thou," known with personal intensity and with communal certitude. I have been struck

with how often the Psalms use the term *baṭaḥ* (security, trust, safety).
Other terms might be studied, but here I suggest that the "Thou" of
the Psalms is the one linked to *baṭaḥ*. The security-giving fidelity of
God is crucial for the faith of the Psalms. It is a word that is used in a
variety of genre, in various ways.

It is used often in the laments. The old "trust" is the basis for
present appeal. In the familiar Psalm 22, former trust is now the
source of hope:

> In thee our fathers *trusted*;
>> they *trusted*, and thou didst deliver them.
> To thee they cried, and were saved;
>> in thee they *trusted*, and were not disappointed (vv. 4–5).

Along with the double use of "trust," notice the poem has "in thee/
thou/to thee/in thee." In Psalm 56, we have a statement of present
confidence which gives the basis for a bold dismissal of threat:

> When I am afraid,
>> I put my *trust* in thee.
> In God, whose word I praise,
>> in God *I trust* without a fear.
> What can flesh do to me? . . .
>> in God *I trust* without a fear.
> What can man do to me? (vv. 3–4, 11).[19]

In Psalm 13, the term is used as a resolution of the Psalm, an assurance of being faithfully dealt with:

> But I have *trusted* in thy steadfast love;
>> my heart shall rejoice in thy salvation.
> I will sing to the Lord,
>> because he has dealt bountifully with me (vv. 5–6).

The double use in Psalm 5 is especially interesting. In v. 4 it is a call
for confidence in Yahweh:

> Offer right sacrifices,
> and put your *trust* in the Lord.

But as the end of the Psalm (v. 8), the same word is used and rendered in the RSV as "safety":

In peace *(shalom)* I will both lie down and sleep;
for thou alone, Oh Lord, makest me dwell in *safety.*

Thus: Put your *trust* in Yahweh/lie down in safety. The "Thou" of Yahweh is fully articulated in this double use of *baṭaḥ*. At the beginning and end and in both uses, it is directly linked to the name of Yahweh.

In Psalm 31, a somewhat more reflective Psalm, the same word is used twice. In v. 6, the trust of Yahweh is contrasted with idols. (Linkage to the first two commandments is suggested and shows how closely linked are *trust* and *obedience*.) And in vv. 14–15, the word bespeaks well-being and confidence:

But I *trust* in thee, O Lord,
I say, "Thou art my God."
My times are in thy hand.

The Psalm thus draws this word of *reassurance* into the realm of theological *polemic*. For the *trust* in this live "Thou" is a repudiation of alternatives not to be trusted. The issue of *trust Yahweh/reject idols* is a fundamental issue for education. It asks if we understand and adhere to the first commandment. Luther has understood better than any other that obedience to the first commandment is not simply a matter of right religion, but a matter of well-being, personal wholeness, and the capacity to live a liberated life. Following Erik Erikson,[20] we have probed in some depth the matter of "basic trust" as a psychological issue. But we have work to do about the theological dimension. The Psalms are concerned with the practice of *trust*, as it refers to the true God and denies the others. The Psalter knows that everything is at stake for personal well-being and social relations in that matter of trust in God.

One other Psalm warrants our attention. Psalm 115 is a doxology to Yahweh. Our word is used as a summons to confess the sovereignty of Yahweh.

O Israel *trust* in the Lord!
He is their help and their shield.
O house of Aaron, put your *trust* in the Lord!
He is their help and their shield.

You who fear the Lord, *trust* in the Lord!
He is their help and their shield (vv. 9–11).

Interestingly, the term is also used at the end of vv. 3–8 as a refutation of idols who are not to be relied upon:

Those who make them are like them;
so are all who *trust* in them.

Thus the summons to trust this "Thou" is a summons away from "no-thous" who cannot keep their promises. The use of "Thou" is not simply a conventional religious statement of trust. It is at the same time a conflicted word that calls for decision among various alternatives. Trust of Yahweh is not only *doxological*, but also *polemical*.

The use of the term is disputed, as is evident in the appeal of Assyria in the speech of 2 Kings 18:19ff.:

On what do you *rest* this *confidence* of yours?[21]
On whom do you now *rely*, that you have rebelled against me?
Behold, you are *relying* now on Egypt, that broken reed
of a staff . . . But if you say to me, "We *rely* on the Lord our
God . . ."

The issue is joined around alternative reliances and alliances.[22] The Assyrians call Israel away from Yahweh. The answer to that temptation is given in the prayer of Hezekiah in 2 Kings 19:15–19, which begins and ends with the same formula:

Thou art the God, thou alone . . .
Thou, O Lord, art God alone.

The double use of *'attah* (Thou) is a strong response to the dispute over *batah* in 18:20ff. The linkage between these Psalms and the political exchange in 2 Kings 18—19 indicates that the issue of trust in this sovereign "Thou" is not simply a religious matter, but has direct implications for decision-making in the arena of social ethics. Thus I suggest that educators have few more important agendas than helping people learn to say "Thou," and to know to whom to say it and to say it with confidence *(batah)*.

Trust, as used in the Psalms, covers an important polarity. It is a polarity we may recover if we are to pursue genuine piety. On the one hand, this is bold, unreserved communion with God, a genuine at-homeness. It is this that leads the Psalmist to say, "The Lord is my portion!" (Ps. 16: 5–6; 73:26; 119:57; 142:5).[23]

> Surely goodness and mercy shall follow me
>   all the days of my life;
> and I shall dwell in the house of the Lord for ever (Ps. 23:6).

> I was glad when they said to me,
>   "Let us go to the house of the Lord" (Ps. 122:1).

There is an eagerness and delight in the Lord who is understood as the resolution of every need and every hope. At the same time, there is an abrasive, political, polemical quality of trust, the taking of a decision, the choosing of sides, the readiness to stand with and there-fore to stand over-against. These two poles are not easy to hold together. But they belong together, insisting that *toughness* and *at-homeness* are both practiced in the presence of this "Thou."

3. The "Thou" who is addressed in the Psalms is one who can be trusted. But who is this "Thou," and how is trust to be experienced and articulated? My urging is this. *Communion* with the God of Israel is understood primarily in terms of *obedience*. There is no communion prior to or apart from obedience. But obedience is the move required for communion. Such a proposal, of course, understands the religion of Israel to be definitionally an ethical religion concerned about social value. There is no pre-ethical religious experience in Israel. It is not only a judgment about the expectations laid upon Israel, but an assertion about the character of Yahweh who has uppermost in his agenda the great public questions of justice and righteousness.

Obedience is the primal form of biblical faith. It follows that obedi-ence belongs to full humanness. That should not surprise us if we reflect on the mission of the gospel, which is to bring all creation to joyous obedience.

Only after I had written thus far on *obedience* after *trust* did it occur to me that "trust and obedience" is a full summary of Israel's part in this relationship. Of course, that is caught simply and succinctly in the gospel hymn, "Trust and obey, for there's no other way, to be happy in Jesus, but to trust and obey."[24] These are not first of all Christian categories, but they are basic for Israel's faith. Education in the church must be unambiguous about obedience as the stuff of biblical faith. That conviction is attested in both Jewish and Christian theology. Abraham Heschel entitles one of his chapter subheadings, "To be is to Obey."[25] He observes that the first word to Adam is a command. Later on Heschel has it this way: "I am commanded—therefore I am":

> Do I exist as a human being? My answer is: *I am commanded—therefore I am*. There is a built-in *sense of indebtedness* in the consciousness of man, an awareness of *owing gratitude*, of being *called upon* at certain moments to reciprocate, to answer, to live in a way that is compatible with the grandeur and mystery of living.[26]

And closer to home, John Calvin parallels this conviction: "But not only faith perfect and in every way complete, but all right knowledge of God is born of obedience."[27]

OBEDIENCE AS EXPERIENCE OF GOD'S NEARNESS

Now, it strikes me that faith as obedience is one way to bring together these divergent elements of the educational task we have considered. I do not doubt that obedience is a main issue for the contemporary church. Obedience is scarcely the first way to talk about religion in our culture. It smacks of authoritarianism and supernaturalism of the crudest kind. But objection to such caricatures of true obedience does not eliminate the affirmation made in all parts of that tradition, in all elements of the canon, that the human creature is not a creature sufficient unto himself/herself, but is the gift of Another, intended for the purposes of another. That, of course, is why the modes of knowledge all across the Bible, as we have seen them, seek to outflank flat, one-dimensional technical positivism. The outflanking is because we deal with a mystery, a compelling mystery, but a mystery whose name we know, so that we call this one

"Thou." It is a mystery whose purpose we know. That is why we obey. But the tradition is multifaceted and varied. Obedience is not one thing, not easily known, surely not to be reduced. The whole canon is needed to explore the fullness of obedience. As the educator must guide into obedience as a mode of knowledge, so the educator must avoid every reductionism.

So my proposal for the various tendencies and nuances we have tried to trace is that they meet in the summons to and expectation for obedience. I should argue that each of the divisions of the canon we have considered speaks in its own distinctive way about an *obedient response to a holy God*. As we shall see, both terms are important. *Obedience* is a willing, ready response to God's purpose. But *holy* means that the purpose is not flat, simple, obvious, or accessible in our terms. Therefore, in the formula *obedience—holiness*, there is still much to be explored. We must face the temptation of reductionism. But again it is evident that reductionism to clarify God's holy will has been going on in the Bible itself. That is, the witness of all these texts is aimed at obedience. Yet it is an obedience not easily articulated.

The aim of full obedience in the Torah will not greatly surprise us. We have understood the Torah in terms of affirmation of a consensus. The point of the Torah is that each new generation should live in that consensus. Thus the question is an attempt to learn what the older generation understands: "What is the meaning of the testimonies and the statutes and the ordinances which the Lord our God has commanded you?" And the answer:

> We were Pharaoh's slaves in Egypt; and the Lord brought us out of Egypt with a mighty hand. . . . And the Lord commanded us to do all these statutes and to fear the Lord our God, for our good always, that he might preserve us alive, as at this day. And it will be righteousness for us, *if we are careful to do all this commandment* before the Lord our God, as he has commanded us (Deut. 6:20–21, 24–25).

The juxtaposition of saving deed and responding obedience is clear. The aim is life-giving righteousness. Israel has come to an awareness that the land will be kept only by obedient righteousness. Israel has learned that obedient righteousness is possible, even in the land so filled with snares. This fundamental claim of the Torah should not be overlooked or minimized simply because it is so well-known to us. In the ancient world and in the contemporary world, this is a distinctive and radical claim. The Torah at its center, in the Sinai tradition and in the preaching of Deuteronomy, makes these staggering claims for social well-being as the cost of the land. The Torah holds the line against every other kind of securing which appears to be available. This part of the canon asserts even in face of self-securing modernity that there is no *secure land* which is apart from Torah obedience. We must probe to learn if we believe that.

In the second part of the canon, the prophets, the issue of obedience is not so simple. Particularly since we have argued that the proclamation of God's new act (of beginnings and endings) is the main point. If that proclamation is the main point, then a stress on repentance and obedience is not central. We have understood the prophets in terms of a break in the consensus, a break which comes from the underside, the voice of those without credentials. And so it is.

But we should insist on two grounds that even in the prophetic "canon of discontinuity," expectation of obedience is central and radical. That is so first of all because the new action of God is never so far removed from the demand of obedience. Each new action of God is in order that God should be fully God, that is, should be fully trusted and obeyed. Second, there is little doubt in the redacting process that stress was increasingly placed on Israel's obedience. The old age is ended in judgment because Israel did not obey (this is a theme especially prominent in Jeremiah; c.f. Jer. 5:21; 7:13; 11:10; 13:10–11; 22:5, 21; 25:4, 8; 29:19; 35:17). The new age is an invitation to a new obedience.

This way of linking obedience to prophetic discontinuity is most apparent in Jeremiah and Ezekiel, who lived most precisely at the point of nullification. On the one hand, it is obedience/disobedience which poses the crucial matter of the land (cf. Jer. 26:3, 13). Radical obedience is the only way that "the end of the land" can be averted.

One might have expected that the coming of the end had nullified the category of obedience. The disappearance of obedience might have come in a surge of anger in which the whole relation is ended, so that God no longer expects or permits obedience. Or alternatively, the disappearance of obedience might have come in a new religion of utter graciousness in which the call for obedience is overcome by God's mercy. But neither is the case. Anger is not decisive and grace is not that free, for the dominant mode of the relationship is between a Lord who will be obeyed and a people who will be obedient. It is a new relation, but this demanding asymmetry persists. This has not changed from the old order to the new age. So the anticipations of Jeremiah and Ezekiel are essentially "Torah-filled."

> I *will put my law within them,* and I will write it upon their hearts; and I will be their God and they shall be my people. And no longer shall each man teach his neighbor and each his brother, saying, "Know the Lord," for they shall all know me, from the least of them to the greatest, says the Lord; for I will forgive their iniquity, and I will remember their sin no more (Jer. 31:33-34).

> A new heart I will give you, and a new spirit I will put within you; and I will take out of your flesh the heart of stone and give you a heart of flesh. And I will put my spirit within you, and *cause you to walk in my statutes and be careful to observe my ordinances.* You shall dwell in the land which I gave to your fathers; and you shall be my people, and I will be your God (Ezek. 36:26-28).

> My servant David shall be king over them; and they shall all have one shepherd. They shall *follow my ordinances and be careful to observe my statutes.* They shall dwell in the land . . . and I will be their God, and they shall be my people (Ezek. 37: 24, 27).

The new age is an utter gift, but a gift which evokes obedience. It is, of course, difficult to determine how much of Jeremiah and Ezekiel has passed through scribal editing in this emphasis. That does not matter greatly for our concern. The point is that as we have it, the waiting of Israel is for a new obedience.[28] It is the contention of the prophetic tradition *as we now have it* that the new age of well-being will be an age of utter obedience. The new age will be characterized by the kind of righteousness that was not practiced in the old time. Thus the prophetic canon appeals to the norms and claims of the

Torah. But it breaks beyond the Torah in promising new power (new heart) for full obedience. The anticipations of the prophets are much more daring than the prescriptions of the Torah.

In the third part of the canon, we may comment particularly on the wisdom traditions (though the Psalms, of course, do not ignore the motif of obedience). The ultimate linkage of *Torah and wisdom* in the late period is a complicated question that need not detain us here.[29] In general, it is correct to say that Torah in Israel comes "from above" and that wisdom comes "from below," that Torah is transparent and precise while wisdom has a dimension of hiddenness and inscrutability to it. They surely do move in different spheres. While Torah may have satisfied public religion, wisdom comes to be the work of intellectually alert and restless people who will not settle for easy, obvious, or conventional positions. We have understood wisdom as the *practice of discernment of the interconnectedness of life* in ways that are not immediately apparent. There is a reflective, contemplative aspect to wisdom that does not want to move quickly to clichés. What is evident is that in the canonical wisdom as now transmitted, there are firm boundaries and limits to speculation. We know from other non-canonical texts that a great deal of speculation went on that moved in the directions of gnosticism, apocalypticism and mysticism. But the traditionalists who decided the canon have kept to a steady vision. Finally, they have understood that genuine *discernment* concerns not *speculation* but the practice of *obedience*. While it may have taken a bold and nervy intellectual effort to bring wisdom and Torah together, it is also the case that from the beginning, there has been an awareness of the commonality of the two enterprises. Moreover, discernment of the secrets of life is not an end in itself, but concerns the life and the will of the life-giver. The secrets of life finally lead to praise of the Creator. *Discernment ends in doxology.* Wisdom is not autonomous in Israel, but refers to the Creator. Thus the wisdom of Israel has a *practicality* to it which takes seriously the demanding character of Yahweh the Lord of wisdom:

> Trust in the Lord with all your heart,
>   and do not rely on your own insight.

In all your ways acknowledge him,
  and he will make straight your paths.
Be not wise in your own eyes;
  fear the Lord, and turn away from evil.
It will be healing to your flesh
  and refreshment to your bones (Prov. 3:5-8).

Wisdom refers to Yahweh. Life comes not from sources ordained in creation, but from the Lord of creation. Therefore wisdom can make a claim for itself that points beyond itself. So wisdom says:

For he who finds me finds life
  and obtains favor from the Lord;
but he who misses me injures himself;
  all who hate me love death (Prov. 8:35-36).

Wisdom probes the mysteries of life and death, but finally always refers them to the sovereign rule of Yahweh.

Now, that does not surprise us in the Book of Proverbs. Let us note that the same inclination is at work in Job and Ecclesiastes where we do not expect it. In the great poem of Job 28, we have seen that in vv. 1-27 there is speech about the mystery of God who keeps wisdom inscrutable. Terrien[30] has identified a refrain in vv. 12-13 and 20-21, and believes a third refrain might have come after v. 27. But instead of such a refrain, in v. 28, we now have this:

And he said to man,
  Behold, the fear of the Lord, that is wisdom,
  and to depart from evil is understanding.

Terrien takes a dim view of the verse, terming it "moralistic thought," "editorially substituted," "conventional." He believes that v. 28 must be removed to let the text have its majestic way. That is possible, but I am unconvinced. I should not use such terms as "conventional." I should term it "characteristically Israelite." It is an Israelite way of setting a limit on intellectual speculation. It is Israel's insistence that after all of the exploration, Israel may obey. It is, as Terrien sees,[31] to descend from heaven to earth, to leave God with his awesome mystery. But it is also to leave humankind with the daily round of decisions, power, and temptations. So even if this is editing,

I should call it Israelite editing of a quite intentional kind which never permits the aesthetic to wander too far from the ethical.[32] Job 28:28, so to speak, at the last comes home to Prov. 3:7. The bold exploration of the poem of Job has not gotten far beyond that fundamental conviction of obedience to Yahweh's Torah. Now that is a theological, not an aesthetic judgment. One can readily agree with Terrien that such a move in v. 28 tends to flatten or terminate the exploration in a not very imaginative way. And perhaps too high a price is paid. But the point made here is that it is a price characteristically paid by Israel who stays close to the summons to obedience. Whether the conclusion of v. 28 is aesthetically appropriate or not, it is characteristically Israelite. The glory of God comes to us as a summons concerning God's holiness and the justice of the neighbor.

We may observe the same process in Ecclesiastes. As is well known, the Preacher moves to the raw edges of faith and flirts with cynicism, even beyond Job. It is generally agreed that 12:13–14 is an editorial "correction" designed to place the whole subversive piece into a more viable context:

> The end of the matter; all has been heard. Fear God, and keep his commandments; for this is the whole duty of man. For God will bring every deed into judgment, with every secret thing, whether good or evil.

Again, the commentators are filled with pejorative adjectives for these verses.[33] Perhaps our response should be left at that, for there is no doubt that these verses take the edge off. But another reading is possible.[34] It is thinkable that these verses mean to link the text to the main claims of the old consensus. That may be only protective orthodoxy, but it may also be a fundamental recognition in Israel that for all such intellectual niceties, there are still reliable forms of obedience. These can be practiced in any context and must indeed be practiced if life is to hold together.[35]

Obedience takes different forms in these different literatures. Obedience may mean the receiving of the *disclosure* that is undoubted (Torah). It may mean participation in the *disruption* that is abrasive (Prophets). Or it may mean the practice of discernment that attends both to the connections and to the incongruities (Wisdom). As one moves from *receiving* to *participation* to *practice*, from Torah to Prophets to Wisdom, the learner becomes more active and takes more initiative. These different modes of obedience must be honored.

Yet, we may observe that in their present form there is also a commonality in obedience which moves through these pieces:

1. In answer to the question, "What do these stones mean?" there is this:

> And the Lord commanded us to do all these statutes, to fear the Lord our God, for our good always, that he might preserve us alive, as at this day (Deut. 6:24).

2. In answer to the question, "Is there a word from the Lord?" there is this:

> And I will put my spirit within you, and cause you to walk in my statutes and be careful to observe my ordinances (Ezek. 36:27).

3. In answer to the question, "Where shall wisdom be found?" there is this:

> Behold, the fear of the Lord, that is wisdom;
> and to depart from evil is understanding (Job 28:28).

> Be not wise in your own eyes;
>   fear the Lord, and turn away from evil (Prov. 3:7).

> Fear God, and keep his commandments; for this is the whole duty of man. For God will bring every deed into judgment, with every secret thing, whether good or evil (Eccles. 12:13–14).

There is a commonality in the tradition that expresses the consensus, breaks the consensus, and broods over the hiddenness. In all these forms, there is still the simple claim of trust and obedience. That should do it.

We must, however, add this one haunting footnote. You may think of others, but the note in Job 42:8 gives us pause about knowing too much about obedience. In this prose ending, which seems to smooth things over, surprisingly it is Job's friends who are termed "foolish." It is Job the restless protester who is commended for speaking what is right. There is at least a hint that not everything has been subsumed

under the consensus. Flat characterizations of obedience are still provisional in the face of the holy God.

We have thus far, from Jer. 18:18, tried to hold clearly to the tripartite canon and the threefold way of Israel's knowledge. But before we
finish, we may observe three counter moves which work against such
a neat division. Finally, the three parts of the canon are not kept so
clearly apart. That is because the *busy redacting processes* witness to
live theological enterprise. Israel could not countenance three witnesses that did not move toward the same God. So the complicated
traditioning process testifies to that theological conviction that these
modes of knowing and *substances of what is known,* are deeply interre-
lated and dependent on each other.

1. We have seen by our attention to Prov. 3:7, Job 28:28, Eccles.
12: 13–14 that there is a *"Torah-izing" process.* The Torah has always
been dominant. The editing process shows the Torah extending its
domination over all the literature, seeking to bring all the texts in line
with the old consensus. The old consensus is unbothered about the
breaks caused by new voices. It is unresponsive to the hiddenness of
wisdom (and to the derivative question of theodicy). It believes that
enough is known for every crisis, enough is known for the anguish of
Job and the cynicism of Ecclesiastes. It holds that in any and every
moment, it is enough to heed the ancient teaching, always enough for
our parents, enough now for us as well, and eventually enough for
our children. If these editors had their way, the other two parts of the
canon would read more like the Torah.[36]

2. But the "Torah-ization" of the Bible is not the only complicating
maneuver. Joseph Blenkinsopp[37] has studied from another perspective the tension between the old commitments of the Torah and the
free authority claimed by the prophets. The prophets, as we have
argued, represent a threat to the old tradition. The Torah, Blenkinsopp argues, must come to terms with the prophetic challenge. One
way of doing this, as we have noted, is the submission of the prophets
to the Torah. This appears to be what happened, for example, in the
Deuteronomic handling of Jeremiah. The other way, to which
Blenkinsopp attends, is to let some of the prophetic claims be present

in the Torah itself. So it is his hypothesis that a central concern of the Torah, as it now stands, is the legitimacy and the limits of prophecy. This is evident in Deuteronomy (especially 18:15–22),[38] in the priestly tradition, and in the conclusion of Deut. 34:10–12.

What happens in this knowing, editing process is that prophecy becomes transformed in ways that permit it to be contained within the tradition. Thus Blenkinsopp can speak variously of "scribal prophecy,"[39] "clerical prophecy,"[40] and "theocratic prophecy."[41] This recasting of prophecy to conform it to tradition, but also to give it its say, is evident not only with reference to the Torah, but also in the writings. Thus for Blenkinsopp, the freedom of the surprising untraditional authority of the prophets is the main problem of the canon. Both Torah and Writings have now been edited in ways to deal with it. In Torah, the figure of Moses stands over the process. In the Writings, it is scribal comment of the tradition which is the new voice of prophecy. The result of such an analysis again is to overcome some of the distance between the parts of the canon. As must always be the case with educators, however, the settlement is uneasy. It yields

an unresolved tension, an unstable equilibrium, between rational order and the unpredictable and disruptive, between the claims of the past and those of the present and the future. When emphasis is placed too much on the former the outcome is likely to be the conferring of absolute validity on present structures, bureaucratic paralysis and a drift to cultural assimilation. When rational order is neglected in favor of the charismatic, the tendency will be towards disunity, disequilibrium and ultimately sectarianism. Prophecy is necessary if only to show up the precarious nature of all fixed order and the claims to legitimacy which sustain them, but prophecy alone cannot build a lasting community. . . . Our study of the canon has led to the conclusion that no one interpretation of the tradition can be accorded final and definite status. The presence of prophecy as an essential part of the canon means that it will always be possible and necessary to remold the tradition as a source of life-giving power.[42]

3. A different consideration about the interrelatedness of the modes of knowledge and the substance of knowledge has been more recently given by Gerald T. Sheppard. It is his contention that "at a certain

period in the development of Old Testament literature, wisdom became a theological category associated with an understanding of canon which formed a perspective from which to interpret Torah and prophetic traditions. In this sense wisdom became a hermeneutical construct for interpreting sacred Scripture."[43]

By a series of careful textual studies of non-canonical texts (Sirach, Baruch), Sheppard shows that in the late Old Testament period, the Torah was restudied in sapiential categories. Reflective of a scribal (that is, textual) consciousness, such study thus legitimates Torah in a contemporary way. That is, all of the Torah is passed through the filter of wisdom.

> Only by grounding wisdom in the interpretation of the superior canonical Torah traditions, could wisdom teachings (both canonical and non-canonical) retain an independent religious significance in any way comparable to that of the Torah in the post-exilic period. Conversely, these wisdom interpretations legitimate the Torah and its claim to pervasive authority by demonstrating in practical terms how Torah narrative directly informs the concerns of wisdom.[44]

It is my urging that as the canon makes these moves to use and authorize each other, so church educators must be able to move back and forth among the modes and substances of the canon, depending on context and intent.

Now, the point of these three comments is to urge that the tripartite canon is a useful place to begin our investigation. But it cannot end there. We have pursued our analysis of the three parts of the canon and have argued that they reflect three ways of presenting Israel's faith. Moreover, each of them serves a distinctive theological and educational function. However, we have indicated:

1. Out of Prov. 3:7, Job 28:28, Eccles. 12:13–14 as well as in texts in Jeremiah and Ezekiel, that the *claims of the Torah* move into the other parts of the canon as well.

2. Following Blenkinsopp, that the *influence of prophetic freedom* is important for understanding Torah and Writings.

3. Following Sheppard, that the *influence of probing wisdom* in the other parts of the canon, especially the Torah, is important.

These arguments set alongside our comments on the Psalms suggest:

1. That trust and obedience to a holy "Thou" is the locus of education.

2. That the literary evidence of that trust and obedience presents a variety of configurations in the literature and in educational practice.

3. That every configuration of literature and educational practice has special links to its context. Each such configuration needs to be assessed, critiqued, and appreciated in relation to that context.

4. Because no single one of these canonical tendencies can override the others, every educational effort which moves from one of these perspectives needs to be assessed, critiqued, and corrected in light of the other tendencies, which also are important to the tradition.

Finally, one more consideration about *obedience to the Holy God.* There is a problem in that formulation, a problem which is crucial for education in the community of faith. It concerns the tension, distance, and slippage between *Holy God* and *obedient people.* We know the meaning of the stones (our first question). However, there is a tendency for those who know the meaning of the stones to collapse the distance and assume a complete match between Holy God and obedient people. While we wait for a word from the Lord (our second question), we are never sure which word is from the Lord. When it comes, we are sometimes offended by it. While we assign wisdom to the Lord, we do not know where or how wisdom will be found (our third question). That is, the second and third parts of the canon do not so easily permit a match between holiness and obedience. Or with reference to Job 28, we do not know completely about the relation between vv. 1–27, the majestic reflection on wisdom's inscrutability, and v. 28 which turns toward obedience to known duties. The question of Israel's faith is the relation between the *mystery of God* that always stands beyond and the *concrete practice of obedience* which must be done daily.

Deut. 4:5–8 both states the problem and provides clues as clearly as any place in Scripture:

Behold, I have taught you statutes and ordinances, as the Lord my
God commanded me, that you should do them in the land which you
are entering to take possession of it. Keep them and do them; for that
will be your wisdom and your understanding in the sight of the peoples, who, when they hear all these statutes will say, "Surely this
great nation is a wise and understanding people." For what great
nation is there that has a god so near to it as the Lord our God is to
us, whenever we call upon him? And what great nation is there that
has statutes and ordinances so righteous as all this law which I set
before you this day?

As is well-known, these verses come in this great and enigmatic
chapter 4, a report on the Horeb encounter. Central to that report is
the invisible freedom of God. A voice was heard, but no form was
seen. God sojourns quite beyond the probing of Israel. The theoph-
any is the disclosure of an unseen God. But the *unseen God is a heard
God.*[45] What is heard of God is commandment. It is not God that is
heard; it is commandment. That slippage is not only problematic,
but definitional for Israel. The *freedom* of God is that there is no
form. The *nearness* of God is a commandment. The *nearness of God* is
a *summons to obedience.*

Now, in our four verses,[46] vv. 5–6a are an appeal for obedience;
linked to the summons is a promise of land. On the close side, commandments belong to the *land*—the concrete, identifiable land of
Israel. But on the far side, commandments are understood as *wisdom.*

. . . that will be your wisdom and understanding . . .
surely this great nation is a wise and understanding
people.

For Israel *commandment* is the middle term of *wise* and *land. Land*
is a very specific concrete mark of Israel. *Wisdom* is a way of discerning things that all peoples can appreciate. Thus the riddle of Israel
among the nations is caught precisely in this notion of commandment. Commandment as discernment is something the nations can
respect, so a place is secured among the nations by obedience. Commandment is also an ingredient of the special relation of Israel to
God, so the land is secured also by covenant.

The text asserts that commandment is definitional for Israel, the middle term of the heard God who is present yet is not seen. Vv. 7–8 offer two rhetorical questions with the same formula:

For what great nation is there, that has . . .
For what great nation is there that has . . .

Israel is celebrated as having two marks which make it distinctive in the world. The two marks of Israel are a *God so near* and a *Torah so righteous.* Our educational task, perhaps, is caught in the delicate and difficult relation between these two. On the one hand, education is *profoundly theological.* We yearn for the young to know how near God is, so near that God hears whenever we call—a God so near that we may say "Thou" with confidence, the utterance of which reshapes life decisively. The nearness of God is a theme forfeited when faith becomes too technical or too moral. There is a piety here which teaches communion with God.

But a Torah so righteous! That also comes with "Thou." It is a demanding, uncompromising, unaccommodated "Thou" who will be heard and answered and obeyed. A Torah so righteous—a Torah with its own vision of the future, its own hope for the marginal, its own gift for the trusting, its own insistence on justice and equity. Education in Deuteronomy is uncompromising on this point. There is no preobedience knowledge of God. There is no Torah-less God, but a God who always meets Israel in Torah.

This is the focus of Horeb—a God so near, a Torah so righteous. Some would like God to be near without all the demands of Torah. Then we would teach an accommodating, reassuring religion. Others would like a Torah so righteous with a focus on demands. Then we could teach a harsh, conditional faith. But the text will not separate the two.

Educators must work (1) to hold the two together, to keep each corrected by the other, and (2) to keep distinction between the two. The Torah is not God, for in our obedience and disobedience this is a God so near. But God is not God without Torah, and if we would know God, it comes by way of obedience. Thus it is clear that we are concerned here not simply with education, but with the God who is the subject of education.

In the characterization of God and the derivative characterization of Israel, the issue is joined. The issue is joined against a *legalism* that reduces God to Torah and against a *romanticism* which wants God without Torah. The issue is joined with every cultural temptation that wants to collapse God into Torah, or Torah into God, or to have one without the other.

No form, but a voice—that is how it is in Job 28. Vv. 1–27 reflect at length on the inaccessibility of God's wisdom to us. Then, abruptly, v. 28 affirms enough is known to get on with vocation. There is a slippage between vv. 1–27. So in Deut. 4:7–8, the righteous Torah is enough for daily obedience. None may assume that the righteousness of the Torah fully penetrates the God who is near. The righteousness of the Torah lets us proceed with confidence in the daily task of obedience. The nearness of God lets us live without knowing and with trusting.

We began this last discussion with the Psalms, and now we shall conclude there. Moving from Deut. 4:5–8 back to the Psalms, first a comment on Psalm 119. This Psalm knows about a God so near and a Torah so righteous. Perhaps Psalm 119, then, is an appropriate stop-ing point:

1. It catches much of the piety of the Psalms.

2. It surely acknowledges the intimate connection between the Torah and the writings which reflect the probing wisdom of Israel.

3. It offers stylized directness in which everything is staked on "Thou."

We single out two verses which summarize our argument:

> But thou art near, O Lord,
> and all thy commandments are true (v. 151).

Again, it is a reflection which juxtaposes *nearness* and *commandments*. The Psalm knows very well that the commandments do not contain Yahweh, for in the Psalm, Yahweh is addressed frequently and directly without commandments.

And I shall walk at liberty,
for I have sought thy precepts (v. 45).

The term "liberty" renders *rahav*, broad space, free space, extra room. The Torah is liberating, not constrictive.

This juxtaposition of *God and commandments*, of *nearness and righteousness*, perhaps is reflected in Jesus' response to the enquiry about eternal life (Mark 10:17–22). "You know the commandments." Then he adds, "Follow me." The commandments are not the sum of discipleship. Beyond the commandments are radical forms of risk and trust, of embrace and departure. Beyond the commandments is the embrace of Holy God. Jesus never imagines that the commandments are the fullness of discipleship. But they are the port of entry. Beyond them lies the impossibility given only in the gospel of the Holy God (v. 27). Education is rallying the community around that faithful evangelical impossibility.

Notes

ABBREVIATIONS

ASR American Sociological Review

ATR Anglican Theological Review

BASOR Bulletin of the American Schools of Oriental Research

BZAW Beihefte zur Zeitschrift für die neutestamentliche Wissenschaft

FRLANT Forschungen zur Religion und Literatur des Alten und Neuen Testaments

HAT Handbuch zum Alten Testament

JAAR Journal of the American Academy of Religion

JBL Journal of Biblical Literature

JR Journal of Religion

JSOT Journal for the Study of the Old Testament

SBT Studies in Biblical Theology

TBü Theologische Bücherei

ThLZ Theologische Literaturzeitung

USQR Union Seminary Quarterly Review

VT Vetus Testamentum

VTSup Vetus Testamentum, Supplements

WMANT Wissenschaftliche Monographien zum Alten und Neuen Testament

ZAW Zeitschrift für die alttestamentliche Wissenschaft

CHAPTER 1

1. For this dynamic in the biblical text, see James A. Sanders's "Adaptable for Life: The Nature and Function of Canon," in *Magnalia Dei: The Mighty Acts of God,* ed. Frank M. Cross, Werner E. Lemke, and Patrick D. Miller, Jr. (Garden City, N.Y.: Doubleday, 1976), pp. 531–60. Sanders's terms are "adaptability and stability" (p. 551). On a broader scale, Peter Berger, *The Sacred Canopy* (Garden City, N.Y.: Doubleday, 1967) has described the "canonical" processes of world construction and world maintenance. "Every society that continues in time faces the problem of transmitting its objectivated meanings from one generation to the next" (p. 21). Sanders is concerned primarily with the literary process, and Berger characterizes the sociological process. It is our argument here that the literary process of canon and the process of socialization need to be seen in relation to each other, if the Bible is to impinge upon church education.

2. See the general summary by J. Kaster, "Education, OT," *The Interpreter's Dictionary of the Bible,* vol. E–J (New York: Abingdon, 1962), pp. 27–34. On one specific aspect of the Old Testament and education, see H.J. Kraus, "Geschichte als Erziehung," in *Probleme Biblischer Theologie,* ed. Hans Walter Wolff (Munich: Kaiser Verlag, 1971), pp. 258–74. Pertinent discussions in the mainstream of Old Testament studies include Gerhard von Rad, *Wisdom in Israel* (New York: Abingdon, 1972), especially chap. 2; R.N. Whybray, *The Intellectual Tradition in the Old Testament,* BZAW 135 (Berlin: Walter de Gruyter, 1974); E. Gerstenberger, *Wesen und Herkunft des sogenannten 'apodikitischen Rechts' im Alten Testament,* WMANT 20 (Neukirchen: Neukirchener Verlag, 1965); and H.J. Hermisson, *Studien zur Israelitischen Spruchweisheit,* WMANT 28 (Neukirchen: Neukirchener Verlag, 1966).

3. Jack L. Seymour, "Contemporary Approaches to Christian Education," *Chicago Theological Seminary Register* 69 (1979): 1–10.

4. For a general treatment of tradition criticism, see Douglas A. Knight, *The Traditions of Israel,* Society of Biblical Literature Dissertation Series 9 (Missoula: University of Montana, 1973).

5. The programmatic statement is by Gerhard von Rad, "The Form-Critical Problem of the Hexateuch," in *The Problem of the Hexateuch and Other Essays* (New York: McGraw-Hill, 1966), pp. 1–78. For a fuller exposition of his thesis, see his *Old Testament Theology,* vol. 1 (New York: Harper and Row, 1962), pp. 105–305.

6. von Rad, *Old Testament Theology,* vol. 2 (New York: Harper and Row, 1965), p. 395, in speaking of Deuteronomy, concludes, "Thus the

process of forming a canon began." That is a common view about the formation of the present literature. But the social process of canon formation lies well behind the present literature of Deuteronomy.

7. J. A. Soggin, "Kultaetiologische Sagen und Katechese im AT," *VT* 10 (1960): 341–47, suggests that the child question reflects a form of catechetical instruction.

8. The dialectic of holding to the old story and receiving new experience into the old story is exceedingly important and exceedingly difficult. From very different perspectives, this point is central for the work of von Rad, "The Problem," in his tracing of the development of the credo, which takes new data into the classic picture; for the work of Sanders, who stresses flexibility as much as stability; and for the social analysis of Berger, *Sacred Canopy.* My argument is that church education has not intentionally taken up the problem both of transmitting the tradition and of keeping it open. On the one hand, the liberal stream of education in the church has largely abandoned the tradition for the sake of experiential learning, and more conservative streams, on the other hand, have presented the canonical story as though it were closed. The dialectic is the major issue. In what follows, I shall show that the tripartite structure of canon services precisely that issue.

9. In commenting generally on canon without special reference to the Bible, Ralph Norman, "Necessary Texts: Pluralism and the Uses of Canon," *Soundings* 61 (1978): 240, makes the case for canon:
   (1) A strong culture will have its story straight.
   (2) Every story that is straight is kept straight by a good set of classic texts.
   (3) Classic texts must be familiar to everybody.
   (4) A strong culture will keep everybody familiar with classic texts.
I know of no better statement of the linkage between canon and education. Israel could not survive in an alien world if it "did not have its story straight" and did not keep the next generation involved with that story. In the same issue in which Norman's article appears, Susan W. Wittig, "Tradition and Innovation," p. 255, states a countertheme to Norman. She claims not that the story is kept straight by the classics, but that "the classics keep the *culture* straight." That is, not only the tradition, but the *community* depends on the canon.

10. See his massive statement, Brevard S. Childs, *Introduction to the Old Testament as Scripture* (Philadelphia: Fortress Press, 1979).

11. See the varied assessments of Childs's work offered in *JSOT* 16 (1980) and Childs's response. For our purposes the main issue is the relative importance of canonical *shape* and canonical *process.*

12. James A. Sanders, *Torah and Canon* (Philadelphia: Fortress Press, 1972).

13. Sanders, "Adaptable for Life."

14. Ronald E. Clements, "Patterns in the Prophetic Canon," in *Canon and Authority*, ed. George W. Coats and Burke O. Long (Philadelphia: Fortress Press, 1977), pp. 42–55.

15. Joseph Blenkinsopp, *Prophecy and Canon* (Notre Dame: University of Notre Dame Press, 1977).

16. Gerald T. Sheppard, *Wisdom as a Hermeneutical Construct*, BZAW 151 (Berlin: Walter de Gruyter, 1980).

17. A fine example of this dialectic is found in Paul D. Hanson, "The Theological Significance of Contradiction within the Book of the Covenant," in *Canon and Authority*, pp. 110–31.

18. See Sheppard, *Wisdom as Hermeneutical Construct*, p. 13, where his thesis is stated. His argument is that the period after the exile offered such a changed epistemological situation that it was the sapiential reinterpretation of the older part of the canon which continued to let it be pertinent and authoritative. That is, authority is not sustained by rigidity, but by responsiveness to the new situation.

19. In his 1976 article, "Adaptable for Life," Sanders addressed himself primarily to the process, in contrast to Childs who, by definition, cannot give primacy to the process. For our purposes the process is important because it is there that the main points of contact occur with the ongoing and contemporary educational process.

20. Childs, *Introduction*, p. 79, indicates a healthy regard for the dynamic process. Indeed, he understands a rigid placing of the text in an identifiable past as a matter of "decanonizing," that is, of denying the text its present authority.

21. Cf. John Bright, "Jeremiah's Complaints: Liturgy or Expressions of Personal Distress," in *Proclamation and Presence*, ed. John I. Durham and J. Roy Porter (London: SCM Press, 1970), p. 211.

22. Wilhelm Rudolph, *Jeremia*, HAT (Tübingen: J.C.B. Mohr, Paul Siebeck, 1958), p. 114, has summarized the most likely possibilities.

23. On the threefold structure of the Old Testament canon, see Sheppard, *Wisdom as Hermeneutical Construct*, pp. 12–15, and Sid Z. Leiman, *The Canonization of Hebrew Scripture* (Hamden, Conn.: Shoe String Press, 1976), especially pp. 70–71, cited by Sheppard. Special attention may be given to Yalkut Shimeoni Tehillim 702, reported by Leiman and noted by Sheppard, which suggests the different response each part of the canon makes to the same theological issue. This particular treatment suggests, as we do here, a different mode of response and a different substance as well.

That the questions of canon are primarily epistemological is evident in Berger, *Sacred Canopy,* chap. 2. It is my urging that church educators must be much more intentional about modes of epistemology. The tripartite canon, I submit, offers alternative ways on the modes and substance of knowledge. I have found it puzzling that Childs does not make more than he does of the tripartite structure of canon, though obviously it is important for Sheppard, a student of Childs. In his book, Sanders appeals to this structure, but I think he does not take full advantage of it for his argument about flexibility and stability.

24. I am glad to acknowledge my debt to James L. Crenshaw for the particular articulation of my thesis in terms of *ethos/pathos/logos.* While the thesis was germinating within me, he provided the three terms around which I have organized the argument.

25. On the interplay of disclosure and concealing as reflected in Prov. 25:2–3, see Glendon Bryce, *A Legacy of Wisdom* (Lewisburg, Pa.: Bucknell University Press, 1979), pp. 142–59. Bryce comments on the verses: "This cryptic utterance stands in sharp antithesis to the repeated affirmations of the self-disclosure of God in the literature of the Old Testament. Paradoxically, it locates the glory of God in the concealment of meaning. Yet this divine action in concealing is not a momentary thing but a purposive act. The statement is all-encompassing and sets before man a mystery that is not confined to a specific time or situation."

CHAPTER 2

1. An additional use in Josh. 22:24 may be mentioned, for the rubric is not different. But the intention of that text is in a different direction and need not concern us.

2. On a possible setting and function for these exchanges of questions and answers, see J.A. Soggin, "Kultaetiologische Sagen und Katechese im AT," *VT* 10 (1969): 341–47.

3. It is precisely the interplay between the generations that concerns Torah. Peter Berger, *The Sacred Canopy* (Garden City, N.Y.: Doubleday, 1967), p. 15, observes, "every society that continues in time faces the problem of transmitting its objectivated meanings from one generation to the next." Michael Fishbane, *Text and Texture* (New York: Schocken Books, 1979), pp. 79–83, shrewdly suggests that this question-answer exchange may reflect not only an opportunity for *instruction,* but a moment of *conflict* in which the younger generation defies and resists the teaching of the older generation and waits to be persuaded. "Deut. 6:20–25 disclosed a tension between two generations' memories, sets of experiences and commitments. It questions the ability of fathers to transmit their laws and faith

to their sons, who see these as alien and do not feel the same responsibility concerning them. . . . The teaching of the fathers in Deut. 6:20–25 is an attempt to involve their sons in the covenant community of the future, and undoubtedly reflects the sociological reality of the settlement in Canaan. The attempt by fathers to transform their uninvolved sons from '*dis*temporaries' to *con*temporaries, that is, time-life sharers, is an issue of supreme and recurrent significance in the Bible."

4. James A. Sanders, "Adaptable for Life: The Nature and Function of Canon," in *Magnalia Dei: The Mighty Acts of God*, ed. Frank M. Cross, Werner E. Lemke, and Patrick D. Miller, Jr. (Garden City, N.Y.: Doubleday, 1976), p. 541, identifies four elements in Israel's canonical process: depolytheizing, monotheizing, Yahwizing, and Israelitizing. New materials could be included in and contained by the fundamental consensus in Israel, but they had to be recast at the points where the main claims of self-understanding were at issue. The canonical process as concerns the next generation is "walking through" the consensus with the children until it becomes habitual.

5. Paul Tournier, *Secrets* (Richmond: John Knox Press, 1965) has observed that the social process of secret always consists in two parts: (1) the *having of a secret* which no one else knows, and (2) the *telling of secret* for the sake of an alliance. That *having* and *sharing* of a secret is at work in the Torah. On secret in special relation to narrative, see Frank Kermode, *The Genesis of Secrecy: On the Interpretation of Narrative* (Cambridge: Harvard University Press, 1979). Kermode explores the peculiar opaqueness of narrative and presents the strange dialectic of proclamation and concealment. The telling of the narrative to an *insider* does not dispel but deepens the secret. Only an outsider exhausts the narrative in a hearing.

6. Canonical material is a gift provided by the community for the sake of the individual. See Berger, *Sacred Canopy*, p. 13. In Israel, that givenness takes the form of the text. Paul Ricoeur, "Naming God," *USQR* 34 (1979): 215–19, has characterized the "textuality" of biblical faith as a distinctive quality of this faith. The "givenness" which lies behind one's faith and one's listening is the text: "This presupposition of the *textuality* of faith distinguishes *biblical* faith ("bible" meaning book) from all others. In one sense, therefore, texts do precede life. I can name God in my faith because the texts preached to me have already named him." This peculiar form of the givenness of life-world as text is especially crucial in the Torah and has important implications for church education grounded in the Torah.

7. See again Ralph Norman, "Necessary Texts: Pluralism and the Uses of Canon," *Soundings* 61 (1978): 240. But even keeping the story straight is

a dynamic process. In order to keep it straight, it must be continually retold. Thus Ricoeur, "Naming God," struggles with the relation of the *written text* and the *spoken word*.

8. Sanders, "Adaptable for Life," p. 535, correctly concludes, ". . . one must insist that a primary definition of Torah cannot be 'law.'" In his article "Torah and Christ," *Interpretation* 29 (1975): 372–90, Sanders helpfully identifies *muthos* and *ethos*, *story* and *ethics*, as the substance of the Torah.

9. Cf. Berger, *Sacred Canopy*, p. 30.

10. In his book, *The Precarious Vision* (Garden City, N.Y.: Doubleday, 1961), Peter Berger describes the crisis faced by persons who live in a well-defined life-world, and then are confronted with a different life-world which is more compelling or appears to be more legitimate. In that crisis, one is forced to redecide between life-worlds and may "switch worlds," as Berger and Thomas Luckmann, *The Social Construction of Reality* (Garden City, N.Y.: Doubleday, 1966), p. 157 suggest. But prior to such a challenge, "our truth" does appear to "the truth." Distance and criticism from "our truth" comes in other parts of the canon, but not in the Torah. The affirmation of "our truth" is likely to be polemical, not only affirming this consensus, but denying and rejecting alternative claims. Thus it is likely in situations of social conflict and of alienation and exile that the matter of canon becomes important, for canon guards against syncretism, that is, mixing "our truth" with "other truth." The recital of this "truth," then, is a political act taken at some risk.

11. To this extent Berger, *Sacred Canopy*, p. 11, is correct in seeing that such "objective reality" is imposed and coercive. There is no negotiation in Israel about the claims of the Torah.

12. In its own way the term *nomos* is even more problematic than is the term *Torah*. *Nomos* will sound to some as a reference to "law" in a legalistic sense. Such is our inheritance from misunderstood Paulinism. But our exegesis may learn a new way from sociology, which understands *nomos* to be the societal order which overrides all personal experiences of disorder. The notion of *nomos* thus can be most helpful in education. In Torah education, the chance is to nurture persons into a sure sense of the orderedness of life, to present a life-world that has coherence, sense, and resilience. David Clines, *The Theme of the Pentateuch*, *JSOT* Sup. 10 (Sheffield: University Press, 1978), p. 102, has seen that every story brings with it a world. The Torah thus presents and creates an ordered world into which persons can be nurtured.

13. See especially Berger and Luckmann, *Social Construction of Reality*. John Westerhoff's understanding of education as socialization is essentially

Torah education. Notice his emphasis on ritual. Taken by itself, Westerhoff's approach is essentially conservative, as is the Torah taken by
itself.

14. Robert Merton, *Social Theory and Social Structure* (Glencoe, Ill.:
Free Press, 1957) chaps. 4 and 5. On story and homecoming, see Charles
E. Winquist, "The Act of Story-Telling and the Self's Homecoming,"
JAAR 42 (1974): 101–13. For Israel's Torah, Winquist's way of putting it is
too removed from historical concreteness, too "transcendental." But his
main point is pertinent to our argument.

15. Stress should be placed here on the importance of language for the
Torah. The process of enculturation depends on the "conversation"
between the articulators of the norms and those who now hear them.
Berger, *Sacred Canopy*, observes that the life-world is sustained by "continuity in conversation." When the conversation is disrupted, the world
totters. That is why Deut. 6:4–9 urges a continuous conversation about
this consensus. On walking and talking, see Paul M. Van Buren, *Discerning
the Way* (New York: Seabury, 1980), p. 13. Van Buren links the biblical
theme of *way* to *conversation*. Education, like theology, is conversation.

16. The literature is prolific. See Clines, *Theme of the Pentateuch*,
pp. 102–11, Sanders, "Torah and Christ," with his emphasis on *muthos*,
and "Adaptability for Life," pp. 535–41; and John Navone, *Towards a
Theology of Story* (Slough: St. Paul Publications, 1977). On p. 42 Navone
observes how story is linked to "homecoming," that is, to a return to a
reliable life-world after experiences of normlessness. Among the most
insightful statements on the theology of story are Robert M. Brown,
"Story and Theology," in *Philosophy of Religion and Theology: 1974 Proceedings of the American Academy of Religion*, pp. 55–72; and James Barr,
"Story and History in Biblical Theology," *JR* 56 (1976): 1–17, now
reprinted in *The Scope and Authority of the Bible*, Explorations in Theology
7 (London: SCM Press, 1980), chap. 1. Recently Gabriel Fackre, *The
Christian Story: A Narrative Interpretation of Basic Christian Doctrine*
(Grand Rapids: Eerdmans, 1978), has attempted to present the fullness of
Christian faith in terms of narrative. G. Ernest Wright, *The Old Testament
and Theology* (New York: Harper and Row, 1969), p. 41, urges that "the
narration of the Bible is not an added or incidental feature of the literature.
It is the indispensable way of presenting Biblical 'truth.' . . ." See also
James B. Wiggins, *Religion as Story* (New York: Harper and Row, 1975);
Robert P. Roth, *Story and Reality* (Grand Rapids: Eerdmans, 1973); James
A. Wharton, "Story, Confession and Theology," *Austin Seminary Bulletin*
90 (1974): 24–56; John Harrell, "Why Storytelling Now?" *Living Light* 13
(1976): 22–29; Ted L. Estess, "Elie Wiesel and the Drama of Interroga-

tion," *JR* 56 (1976): 18–35. See especially the symposium on story in *Theology Today* 32 (1975) with articles by Stroup and Cone, Wiggins, TeSelle, and a more recent statement by Brown. R.J. Coggins, "History and Story in Old Testament Study," *JSOT* 11 (1979): 36–46, offers a critical assessment of the category of story in Old Testament scholarship.

17. The scandalous particularity of Torah education is important if church education is to have authority and staying power. Clifford Geertz, "Religion as a Cultural System," in *Anthropological Approaches to the Study of Religion*, ed. Michael Banton (London: Tavistock Publications, 1966), p. 1, quotes George Santayana, *Reasons in Religion* (1905–06): "Any attempt to speak without speaking any particular language is not more hopeless than the attempt to have a religion that shall be no religion in particular. . . . Thus every living and healthy religion has a marked idiosyncrasy. Its power consists in its special and surprising message and in the bias which that revelation gives to life. The vistas it opens and the mysteries it propounds are another world to live in; and another world to live in—whether we expect ever to pass wholly over into it or not—is what we mean by having a religion."

18. The practice of imagination belongs to both the work of *canon* and the work of *education*. It belongs to canon because the text refuses to be linked to a single setting and always breaks Israel toward new responses to new possibilities. It belongs to *education* because the task of Torah education is that these stories should be the materials out of which new lifeworlds are still to be constructed. Gerald T. Sheppard, *Wisdom as a Hermeneutical Construct*, BZAW 151 (Berlin: Walter de Gruyter, 1980), p. 114, has pointed to this aspect of canon: "In sum, this exegetical exercise operates within the literary and linguistic restrictions of the canonical text and thrives in direct proportion to the artistry and imagination which the interpreter can bring to the task." In a different way, Fishbane, *Text and Texture*, p. 140, comments on the power of the Exodus paradigm in the Torah to evoke new futures: "The simultaneous capacity of the exodus paradigm to elicit memory and expectation, recollection and anticipation, discloses once again its deep embeddedness as a fundamental structure of the biblical historical imagination. But it further discloses just what is so variously and diffusely indicated elsewhere in the Bible; namely that the events of history are prismatic openings to the transhistorical. Indeed, the very capacity of a historical event to generate future expectation is dependent on the transfiguration of that event by the theological intuition that in it and through it the once and future power of the Lord of history is revealed. Without such a symbolic transformation, the exodus would never have given birth to hope. It is the practice of such imagination that turns the

Torah from memory to anticipation." In another context, Fishbane (p. 125) comments on the connection made in the poetry of Exodus 15 between the exodus and the conquest: "And yet it is precisely these rhetorical links between the parts that disclose the layering of Israel's historical consciousness, a layering which fits new events to the archetypal armature of its formative experiences. Deeply constitutive of its reflective imagination, this process predisposed Israel's projective imagination as well." The nurture of "projective imagination" is of major importance for education in the church. In two related articles, Paul Ricoeur comments on the centrality of imagination for faith and for education. In "The Language of Faith," *USQR* 28 (1973): 213–24, reprinted in *The Philosophy of Paul Ricoeur*, ed. Charles E. Reagan and David Steward (Boston: Beacon Press, 1978), he writes: "But the question that I pose to myself, then, is this: What are the place and origin of *possibility?* Faced with this ascetic of necessity, I see the moment in the other hermeneutics when I encounter the problem of what I will call the grace of imagination, the surging up of the possible: how is man a possible, not a necessary reality. . . . I believe that the fundamental theme of Revelation is this awaking and this call, into the heart of existence, of the imagination of the possible. The possibilities are opened before man which fundamentally constitute what is revealed. . . . Consequently, the circle of the atheistic hermeneutics recloses on the necessary, but the circle of the kerygmatic hermeneutics opens on the generation of possibility in the heart of imagination of our language . . . Is not the Good News the instigation of the *possibility* of man by a creative word?" (pp. 237–38). In his comments on the parables of Jesus, "Listening to the Parables of Jesus," *Criterion* 13 (1974): 18–22, also reprinted in *The Philosophy of Paul Ricoeur*, pp. 239–45, he writes: "The Gospel says nothing about the Kingdom of Heaven, except that it is like . . . It does not say what it *is,* but what it looks like. This is hard to hear because all our scientific training tends to use images only as provisory devices and to replace *images* by *concepts.* We are invited to proceed the other way . . . No translation in abstract language is offered, only the violence of a language which, from the beginning to the end, *thinks through* the metaphor and never *beyond.* The power of the language is that it abides to the end *within* the tension created by the images . . . To listen to the Parables of Jesus, it seems to me, is to let one's imagination be opened to the new possibilities disclosed by the extravagance of these short dramas. If we look at the Parables as at a word addressed first to our imagination rather than to our will, we shall not be tempted to reduce them to mere didactic devices, to moralizing allegories. We will let their poetic power display itself within us . . . Poetic means more than poetry as a literary genre. Poetic means creative.

And it is the heart of our imagination that we let the event happen, before we may convert our heart and tighten our will." What Ricoeur says of the parables is decisively true of the Torah stories, as Fishbane suggests. Attention to imagination as a key factor in faithful interpretation is not a new discovery. It was noted already by Spinoza: "Scripture does not explain things by their secondary causes, but only narrates them in the order and the style which has most power to move men, and especially uneducated men, to devotion; and therefore it speaks inaccurately of God and of events, seeing that its object is not to convince the reason, but to attract and lay hold of the imagination." Quoted by John H. Hayes, *An Introduction to Old Testament Study* (New York: Abingdon, 1979), p. 110. Unfortunately Hayes does not provide specific documentation. Concerning imagination and church education, see especially Horace Bushnell, "Our Gospel: A Gift to the Imagination," in *Building Eras in Religion* (New York: Charles Scribner's Sons, 1910), pp. 249–85. I am grateful to Sharon Parks for calling this to my attention. Bushnell is of course recognized as crucial for church education. But his probes in this area have been generally neglected. My colleague, Ruby Schroeder, has pointed out to me a specific statement by Bushnell in that essay which links story and imagination: "It is the consensus on which stories are based that defines the arena for free imagination."

19. Just as the stories are liberating acts of *imagination*, so they are also defiant acts of *politics*. They invite the listener to live in the "world" of this community and from the "truth" of this community, and so to defy and to delegitimate every other "world" and every other "truth." Thus Sheila Collins, "Theology in the Politics of Appalachian Women," in *Woman Spirit Rising*, ed. Carol P. Christ and Judiah Plaskow (New York: Harper and Row, 1979), p. 153, writes: "The Hebrews told their stories as a conscious political act in order to define themselves over against the other cultures of their day. The early Christians who preserved the stories of Jesus paid for these political acts with their lives. They told the story of Jesus in such a way as to set him over against the imperial emperor-worshiping cult of Rome." The Torah draws a line against every alternative reality. That is why Johannes Metz calls these stories "dangerous remembrance." Cf. J. Moltmann, *The Crucified God* (New York: Harper and Row, 1974), p. 5. But Collins understands also that the continuation of these stories as powerful requires continued imagination: "Subversive language, however, must be constantly reinvented, because it is continually being co-opted by the powerful." Moltmann, *The Experiment Hope* (Philadelphia: Fortress Press, 1975), p. 103, quotes Herbert Marcuse: "The memory of the past can allow dangerous insights to arise and the estab-

lished society seems to be afraid of the subversive content of memories."

20. Berger, *Sacred Canopy*, p. 19, observes that the stories, life-world, *nomos*, serve to "order experience." Experience will surely be experienced according to some order and norm if it is at all meaningful. The Torah is a battle for this way of ordering against alternative orders.

21. On story itself as the point, see Hans Frei, *The Eclipse of Biblical Narrative* (New Haven: Yale University Press, 1974).

22. Norman Gottwald, *The Tribes of Yahweh* (Maryknoll, N.Y.: Orbis Books, 1979), p. 121, 736–37, n. 148. See also p. 799, n. 637, in the reference to J. Dus.

23. H. H. Schmid, "Rechtfertigung als Schöpfungsgeschehen," in *Rechtfertigung*, ed. J. Friedrich, W. Pöhlmann, and P. Stuhlmacher (Göttingen: Vandenhoeck and Ruprecht, 1976), p. 403, following Käsemann, treats these three statements as close synonyms.

24. It is precisely the "break" that is so difficult to explicate. Every attempt to "explain" the break falls into the trap of antecedents, the very point the text means to avoid. Cogent comments on the sociological dimension of the break are offered by Gottwald, *Tribes of Yahweh*. But finally we are driven to the category of revelation and disclosure. That will not be "explained," only narrated. Explanations are in order if connections to antecedents can be given. In the absence of those, narrative is a peculiarly appropriate form of expression.

25. Different settlements of the question of antecedents are, of course, offered in the Bible itself. The hypothetical sources JEP, among other things, offer alternative settlements of the question. Cf. Exod. 3:14; 6:2–3.

26. Sanders, "Torah and Christ," p. 380, puts this succinctly: "Torah means the Jewish gospel which, in dialogue with the ongoing believing community of Jews, wherever they might be, gives Jews both identity and a basic understanding of obedience." That the Torah is dominated by the gospel of liberation in the Exodus is fully appreciated by Northrop Frye, "The Critical Path," in *In Search of Literary Theory*, ed. Morton W. Bloomfield (Ithaca, N.Y.: Cornell University Press, 1972), pp. 104–14. Frye speaks first of the "myth of concern" which is present in every culture and may be analagous to Berger's "sacred canopy." Then he observes that in Israel, the central myth of concern is "a revolutionary myth, a myth of freedom." He suggests this myth of freedom with its accompanying belief in a unique historical revelation is at the basis of every western revolutionary movement. That the myth of concern is subordinated to the myth of freedom is crucial for understanding the Torah as gospel. See pp. 133–34, where the myth of freedom is especially linked to the practice of imagination.

27. On the process of the community giving identity to individuals, see

Berger and Luckmann, *Social Construction of Reality,* pp. 129–37. Though he uses different language, Sanders, "Torah and Christ," p. 378, also talks about identity and the process of primary socialization in the Torah.

28. Martin Buber, *Moses* (London: East and West Library, 1956), p. 75, uses this precise terminology.

29. On the use of the term "ethos," see especially Sanders, "Torah and Christ," in which the term is linked to law, ethics, and especially life style. It refers to a life-world and a context in which people live. Education in the Torah is the nurture in and bestowal of an ethos. See Merton, *Social Theory and Social Structure,* p. 461, where he characterizes ethos as a "cultural base." See the bibliographical items, p. 551, n. la.

30. Ricoeur, "The Language of Faith," p. 237, speaks of this as the "surging up of the possible." The question permitted by this tradition, in the words of Ricoeur, is: "How is man a possible and not a necessary reality?" Such a question draws close to what the Bible means by the miraculous.

31. The phrase "core tradition" is that of Walter Harrelson, "Life, Faith and the Emergence of Tradition," in *Tradition and Theology in the Old Testament,* ed. Douglas A. Knight (Philadelphia: Fortress Press, 1977), pp. 18–30. In his observation that the core tradition has a "revolutionary character," Harrelson is close to the categories of Frye's "myth of freedom." Thus Harrelson and Frye comment on the same dimension of Israel's faith from within and from without.

32. Marx's well-known summary of this insight is: "The criticism of heaven is thus transformed into the criticism of earth, the criticism of religion into the criticism of law, and the criticism of theology into the criticism of politics." Cf. David McLellan, *The Thought of Karl Marx: An Introduction* (London: Macmillan Press, 1971), p. 22.

33. In a very different frame of reference, Lewis J. Sherrill has written on *The Gift of Power* (New York: Macmillan Co., 1957) as a way of thinking about church education. While the phrase may be taken less romantically than Sherrill has done, that is precisely correct. Torah education is the bestowal of the gift of power.

34. Ricoeur, "The Language of Faith," p. 235, has nicely joined the two tasks in this statement on Second Isaiah: "Long ago this was the task of Second Isaiah when he tied the preaching of Yahweh to the fight against the Baals, and consequently linked iconoclasm to preaching." Ricoeur has summarized the "unmasking work" in "The Critique of Religion," in *The Philosophy of Paul Ricoeur,* pp. 213–22. This two-sided work of interpretation is fully developed in *The Conflict of Interpretations* (Evanston: Northwestern University Press, 1974).

35. James Sanders, *Torah and Canon* (Philadelphia: Fortress Press,

1972), pp. 26–30. His treatment derives from von Rad, but he has developed particular elements over which von Rad did not linger.

36. See Joseph Blenkinsopp, *Prophecy and Canon* (Notre Dame: University of Notre Dame Press, 1977), pp. 80–85.

37. Sanders, "Adaptable for Life," pp. 550–52, observes that the Torah is "all pre-Conquest. But it is precisely a Torah that would have offered life to a dispersed Israel, a transforming Israel, an emerging Judaism." That is, it is peculiarly appropriate to a people in exile. On the "landless" character of the Torah, see Sanders, *Torah and Canon*, pp. 1–30, and Walter Brueggemann, *The Land* (Philadelphia: Fortress Press, 1977), chaps. 3 and 4.

38. Clines, *Theme of the Pentateuch*, pp. 111–18, which, like most of our work, appeals to the insight of von Rad. See the last paragraph of Gerhard von Rad, *The Problem of the Hexateuch and Other Essays* (New York: McGraw-Hill, 1966), p. 78. See also Brevard Childs, *Introduction to the Old Testament as Scripture* (Philadelphia: Fortress Press, 1979), pp. 128–32: "In spite of a complex development within the tradition of the promise to the patriarchs . . . , the continuing thread which ties together the material is the promise of a posterity and a land." On Torah as a source of hope, see the comments of Fishbane, *Text and Texture*, chap. 6.

39. The phrase is from W. Malcolm Clark, "A Legal Background to the Yahwist's use of 'Good and Evil' in Genesis 2–3," *JBL* 88 (1969): 278.

40. Note again Abraham J. Heschel, *Who is Man?* (Stanford: Stanford University Press, 1965), p. 111.

41. Bernhard W. Anderson, "From Analysis to Synthesis: The Interpretation of Genesis 1—11," *JBL* 97 (1978): 37–39.

42. A major task awaiting Christian theology and Christian education is the recovery of that Jewish tradition of theology which articulates the weakness and vulnerability of God. To be sure, it is present in Christian theology in the theme of the cross. But it is much more poignantly presented in some forms of Jewish theology. See, for example, Byron L. Sherwin, "Elie Wiesel and Jewish Theology," in *Responses to Elie Wiesel*, ed. Harry James Cargas (New York: Persea Books, 1978), pp. 133–49. Such an educational theme has important implications for the nurture of new, faithful personhood. In his dialogue with Jewish faith, Van Buren, *Discerning the Way*, p. 77, quotes this remarkable statement from Gregory of Nyssa: "The one thing which really befits God's nature is to come to the aid of those in need."

43. Note that the theme of "not hearing" is already articulated in Gen. 3:8, 10, where the theme of "voice" is often lost in translation when rendered "sound." Ricoeur has especially understood that listening is an acknowledgment that one is not self-grounded. He writes, "Naming God,"

USQR 34 (1979): 219: *"Listening excludes founding oneself"* (italics in original).

44. On the cruciality and pervasiveness of the promise, see Claus Westermann, *The Promises to the Fathers* (Philadelphia: Fortress Press, 1981).

45. This point is clearly made by Walter Harrelson, *The Ten Commandments and Human Rights* (Philadelphia: Fortress Press, 1980), pp. 54–61. While the ancient intent may have been a polemic against other gods, in our day the same command is a polemic against the notion that there is no god.

46. H. Graf Reventlow, *Gebot und Predigt im Dekalog* (Gütersloh: Gerd Mohn, 1962), pp. 26–28, has urged that the "first command" is not at all a command or an imperative. Rather, it is an exclamation of triumph which provides the basis for the commands to follow.

47. Cf. Brueggemann, *Land*, chap. 4.

48. Cf. Ernest Becker, *Escape from Freedom* (New York: Free Press, 1978), p. 88.

49. Mary Douglas, *Implicit Meanings* (Boston: Rutledge and Paul, 1975), chap. 17, has argued the interesting point that even the dietary laws and the distinctions of clean and unclean in the Priestly materials of the Torah serve to draw distinctions between outsiders and insiders, and to maintain the boundaries essential to the maintenance of a community in exile. Thus even these most difficult laws function in terms of nurture in a specific lifeworld.

50. We have not paid great attention to the ritual aspects of the Torah, but they are, of course, exceedingly important in the socialization process. Suzanne Langer, *Philosophy in a New Key* (Cambridge: Harvard University Press, 1957), p. 153, characterizes ritual as "a disciplined rehearsal of 'right attitudes,'" which yields anchorage, orientation, meaningfulness, a sense of order. The Torah, as often as the child's question is posed, is a "disciplined rehearsal."

CHAPTER 3

1. Primary impetus for this view has come from Gerhard von Rad, especially in the structure of the two volumes of his *Old Testament Theology.* He structured these volumes so that the first is a statement of the Torah tradition, and the second volume, which is on the prophets, is a study in continuity and discontinuity in relation to the data of the first volume. The shift in scholarship since von Rad's study is evident in two studies by Ronald Clements. In the first, *Prophecy and Covenant,* SBT 43 (Naperville: Alec. R. Allenson, 1965), the main argument concerns the relation of the prophets to the tradition. In the second, *Prophecy and Tradi-*

tion (Richmond: John Knox Press, 1975), Clements indicates a rethinking of the matter. The rethinking is not that of Clements, but of the movement of scholarship which he chronicles. There are a number of derivative studies on the prophetic linkage to the tradition, for example, Walter Brueggemann, *Tradition for Crisis* (Richmond: John Knox Press, 1968), chap. 2.

2. Walther Zimmerli, "Prophetic Proclamation and Reinterpretation," in *Tradition and Theology in the Old Testament* (Philadelphia: Fortress Press, 1977), pp. 69–100. See also Werner H. Schmidt, *Zukunftsgewissheit und Gegenwartskritik*, Biblische Studien 64 (Neukirchen: Neukirchener Verlag, 1973). See also Jacob B. Agus, "The 'Yes' and the 'No' of Revelation," in *God and His Temple*, ed. Lawrence E. Frizzell (South Orange, N.J.: Seton Hall University, 1981), pp. 10–19, especially pp. 14–15.

3. If the church wishes to continue education in the prophetic tradition, then it will need, among other things, to work with a "hermeneutic of suspicion." Paul Ricoeur has summarized the matter most helpfully. See especially, "The Critique of Religion," in *The Philosophy of Paul Ricoeur*, ed. Charles E. Reagan and David Steward (Boston: Beacon Press, 1978), chap. 14, where he shows the interrelatedness of "demystification" and "demythologization." Obviously such an undertaking in the church in America will be a demanding and risky one, especially for churches who are committed primarily to the socialization process which seeks to consolidate a consensus.

4. The reader should note the interpretive move made here in the shift from "the end of the world" to "the end of the life-world." I am not sure if these are equivalent. But I suggest this is a helpful way to understand the negative response of the kings to the prophets. We cannot know what the prophets intended ontologically, but at least they were announcing the end of the life-world to which the kings were committed and upon which they relied and from which they benefited. Prophetic criticism concerns critique of a "life-world" which has been absolutized and placed beyond criticism.

5. The tension between Torah and prophets, that is, between the *old consensus* and the *shatterers of the consensus*, is intensified in the conflict of Jesus with the law and especially with the teachers of the law. Jesus' prophetic radicalism is that he undertakes a major criticism of the consensus of the Torah. See James M. Robinson, *The Problem of History in Mark* (London: SCM Press, 1957), chap. 4. Especially in his healing on the sabbath and in his eating with the unqualified, Jesus makes an assault on the consensus and endangers that entire life-world. The issue is joined precisely in Mark 1:22; 11:27–33. The problem is between *established*

authority and *new* authority which can appeal to no such establishment. In the Old Testament, Jeremiah is something of a paradigm for this dilemma in Israel about authority. Cf. Sheldon H. Blank, "The Prophet as Paradigm," in *Essays in Old Testament Ethics*, ed. James L. Crenshaw and John T. Willis (New York: KTAV, 1974), pp. 111-30.

6. See a summary on this issue by Walter Brueggemann, "The Epistemological Crisis of Israel's Two Histories," in *Israelite Wisdom*, ed. John G. Gammie (Missoula, Mont.: Scholars Press, 1978), pp. 85-105.

7. On "state truth," see M. I. Steblin-Kanenskii, *The Saga Mind* (Odense: University Odense, 1973), p. 46.

8. On the matter of "old truth" and "new truth," see John J. Miles, Jr., "Gagging on Job, or the Comedy of Religious Exhaustion," *Semeia* 7 (1977), especially pp. 99-113. While Miles is about other matters and does not intend to comment on the political role and function of old and new truth, I believe there is more implicit in Miles's argument than he himself attends to. That is, even if it is a literary analysis, commitment to "old truth" carries with it conservative political implications. In the case of Miles, the "old truth" implies the common theology of the ancient Near East which is in tension with Israel's scandalous liberation faith. One must be suspicious of every "old time religion," even in the ancient world. See Miles's (p. 119) surprising trade-off of "subversive" for "imperialistic."

9. See David Halberstam, *The Best and the Brightest* (New York: Random House, 1972). It turned out that "the best and the brightest" were those who could manipulate the public instruments of "intelligence" to fashion their own version of reality. It is a mockery when the word "intelligence" refers to such deception and even self-deception. On such knowing and lack of knowing, Jer. 4:22 is not irrelevant.

10. E. Jüngel, "The Truth of Life: Observations on Truth as the Interruption of the Continuity of Life," in *Creation, Christ and Culture*, ed. Richard W. A. McKinney (Edinburgh: T. & T. Clark, Ltd., 1976), pp. 231-36. While Jüngel does not consider the prophets, he makes a christological point not unrelated to our argument.

11. Paul Lehmann, *The Transfiguration of Politics* (New York: Harper and Row, 1975), pp. 48-70.

12. The standard summary is that of J. Lindblom, *Prophecy in Ancient Israel* (Philadelphia: Muhlenberg Press, 1962), which in turn was informed by the older work of Gustav Hölscher. See Ronald Clements, *One Hundred Years of Old Testament Interpretation* (Philadelphia: Westminster Press, 1976), pp. 56-63. Gerhard von Rad, *Old Testament Theology*, vol. 2 (New York: Harper and Row, 1965), pp. 62-69, seeks to relate these phenomeno-

logical matters to more theological concerns. See the more recent summary of Robert R. Wilson, *Prophecy and Society in Ancient Israel* (Philadelphia: Fortress Press, 1980), pp. 21–51.

13. Wilson has made an important move beyond the earlier psychological studies by showing that whatever happened psychologically, it cannot be understood as a personal subjective experience apart from the social context. It is the community of support and legitimation which permits and defines such experiences. Wilson's treatment is altogether commendable, but in my judgment does not go far enough. Every psychology is sociologically sanctioned and legitimated. This surely is a matter needing attention in relation to the prophets.

14. The data is summarized by Patrick D. Miller, Jr., *Genesis 1–11, JSOT* Sup. 8 (Sheffield: University Press, 1978), chap. 1.

15. See the summary comment of James F. Ross, "The Prophet as Yahweh's Messenger," in *Israel's Prophetic Heritage*, ed. Bernhard W. Anderson and Walter Harrelson (New York: Harper and Brothers, 1962), pp. 98–107, and the more recent statement of Kirsten Nielsen, *Yahweh as Prosecutor and Judge, JSOT* Sup. 9 (Sheffield: University Press, 1978). Nielsen offers an extensive bibliography.

16. Martin Luther King, Jr., "I Have a Dream . . . ," *Representative American Speeches* (1963–64): 43–48. Craig Dykstra has suggested this function makes King a new Torah figure because he found a new consensus. Such a parallel to Moses' function is supported by the analysis of James H. Smylie, "On Jesus, Pharaohs, and the Chosen People," *Interpretation* 24 (1970): 74–91. But I suggest that King is better understood as a new voice which shatters a consensus.

17. See a summary report, *New York Times*, 5 April 1968.

18. Wilson, *Prophecy and Society*, has attempted a general synthesis of the present state of that question. No doubt much more work remains to be done in this area. See also Robert P. Carroll, *When Prophecy Failed* (New York: Seabury, 1979), which is an attempt to make use of other contemporary sociological categories for epistemology.

19. Karl Mannheim, *Ideology and Utopia* (New York: Harcourt, Brace and Co., 1936).

20. Jürgen Habermas, *Knowledge and Human Interests* (Boston: Beacon Press, 1971).

21. Peter Berger, "Charisma and Religious Innovation: The Social Location of Israelite Prophecy," *ASR* 28 (1963): 940–50; see the response of James G. Williams, "The Social Location of Israelite Prophecy," *JAAR* 37 (1969): 153–65, and the comment of Wilson, *Prophecy and Society*, pp. 8–10. See the excellent discussion of prophecy and social location by

Robert B. Coote, *Amos Among the Prophets* (Philadelphia: Fortress Press, 1980), especially pp. 24–45. Coote studies Amos in particular, but the implications for prophecy in general are clear.

22. Wolff's first effort in this direction was "Hoseas geistige Heimat," *ThLZ* 81 (1956): 83–94, reprinted in his *Gesammelte Studien zum Alten Testament*, TBü 22 (Munich: Kaiser Verlag, 1973), pp. 232–50. This was followed in 1964 by his most influential *Amos' geistige Heimat*, WMANT (Neukirchen: Neukirchener Verlag, 1964), translated as *Amos the Prophet* (Philadelphia: Fortress Press, 1973).

23. Hans Walter Wolff, "Micah the Moreshite—The Prophet and his Background," in *Israelite Wisdom*, pp. 77–84. See the fuller presentation by Wolff, "Wie verstand Micha von Moreschet sein Prophetisches Amt?" VTSup 29 (1977): 403–17.

24. Wilson, *Prophecy and Society*, pp. 38–39, 69–73, and *passim*.

25. In ibid., pp. 69–73, Wilson offers a summary of the social functions of the peripheral prophets. It includes maintenance of social stability on occasion, but more often concerns innovation and social change. Of course it is not difficult to see why speakers from such contexts would advocate and implement social change.

26. It is again von Rad who articulated this in its most influential form. See also G. Ernest Wright, *The Old Testament and Theology* (New York: Harper and Row, 1969), especially chap. 2. On the criticism of this position, see especially James Barr, *Old and New in Interpretation* (London: SCM Press, 1966) and Brevard S. Childs, *Biblical Theology in Crisis* (Philadelphia: Westminster Press, 1970).

27. See the brief summary of the major literature by Wilson, *Prophecy and Society*, pp. 8–10.

28. On the imaginative function of the prophets, see Walter Brueggemann, *The Prophetic Imagination* (Philadelphia: Fortress Press, 1978).

29. See especially Paul Ricoeur, "The Language of Faith," *USQR* 28 (1973): 231–38. Ricoeur makes an important linkage between imagination and the good news of the kerygma.

30. Ricoeur, "Listening to the Parables of Jesus," *Criterion* 13 (1974): 242, notes the crisis and possibility of language which stays with images and metaphors and refuses to be translated into concepts. The translation of religious metaphor into concepts is a main temptation of the "managerial mentality." That in turn yields an "administrable rationality," the very thing the prophets assault.

31. Northrop Frye, "The Critical Path: An Essay on the Social Context of Literary Criticism," in *In Search of Literary Theory*, ed. Morton W. Bloomfield (Ithaca, N.Y.: Cornell University Press, 1972), p. 192, has char-

acterized the world of imagination as "the holiday or Sabbath world where we rest from belief."

32. The most prominent exception is, of course, Isaiah. Von Rad, *Old Testament Theology*, vol. 2, pp. 146–75, has argued that Isaiah is singularly informed by the traditions of Jerusalem and David and not by the Mosaic liberation tradition. Sociologically he is thus placed in a different socioeconomic setting.

33. The social theory of Peter Berger, *The Sacred Canopy* (Garden City, N.Y.: Doubleday, 1967) and Peter Berger and Thomas Luckmann, *The Social Construction of Reality* (Garden City, N.Y.: Doubleday, 1966) is essentially conservative. That is, they are interested in the formation, construction, and maintenance of a life-world. They see the formation of a "plausibility structure" that is kept viable by the ongoing "conversation" about it as a primary social task. Implicit in their argument is the prospect of deformation and delegitimation, also wrought by words, words which unmask and debunk. The conservative, constructive tendency of their argument is more appropriate to our earlier discussion of Torah. But the countertheme implicit in their argument is pertinent to the second part of the canon. Thus they can speak of the "transformation" of social reality which amounts to an action which "switches worlds" (cf. *Social Construction of Reality*, pp. 156–57). Peter Berger, *The Precarious Vision* (Garden City, N.Y.: Doubleday, 1961), especially chap. 11, has pursued this negating and/or liberating process.

34. This argument, which is embodied in classic liberal Protestantism, is especially championed by Georg Fohrer, "Remarks on Modern Interpretation of the Prophets," *JBL* 80 (1961): 319: "This shows that the true end of prophecy was to turn the sinful man of that day to repentance or redemption and thereby to effect the salvation of lost man . . . they admonish us all to return to the one God and receive redemption." See the response of Werner H. Schmidt, *Zukunftsgewissheit und Gegenwartskritik*, Biblische Studien 4 (Neukirchen: Neukirchener Verlag, 1973), with his strong stress on future as critic of the present.

35. This is the presupposition of much of the scholarship related to the work of von Rad, Westermann, and Wolff. Claus Westermann, *Basic Forms of Prophetic Speech* (Philadelphia: Westminster Press, 1967), pp. 81–89, concludes from this review of form critical study that the admonition, call to repentance, and warning are secondary to prophetic speech forms. The prophetic thrust is not a call to human repentance, but an announcement of God's new intrusion.

36. See the measured summary and judgment of Thomas M. Raitt, *A Theology of Exile* (Philadelphia: Fortress Press, 1977), chap. 2, and his

detailed analysis, "The Prophetic Summons to Repentance," *ZAW* 83 (1971): 30–49.

37. On change that is not coercive but permissive of real newness, see Paul Ricoeur, "The Language of Faith," reprinted in *The Philosophy of Paul Ricoeur*, ed. Charles E. Reagan and David Stewart (Boston: Beacon Press, 1978), especially pp. 236–38. On newness as characteristic of God, see M. Douglas Meeks, *Origins of the Theology of Hope* (Philadelphia: Fortress Press, 1974), pp. 80–89.

38. A good example of prophetic faith interpreted to mean human possibility is in Harvey Cox, *On Not Leaving it to the Snake* (New York: Macmillan Co., 1967). The issue is more directly put in his article, "Tradition and the Future II," *Christianity and Crisis* 27 (1967): 227–31, which approaches the prophetic as a statement about human possibility. It is evident in retrospect that the recent secular theology really urged human capability as the hope. Whereas Cox distinguishes between prophetic faith which celebrates human responsibility and apocalyptic faith which bespeaks human abdication, a very different notion of prophecy is here urged, which announces the new actions of God, independent of human choice and activity. Cox's portrayal of the prophets is, I judge, too anthropocentric.

39 On the tradition-history of the phrase, see Robert Bach, "Bauen und Pflanzen," in *Studien zur Theologie der alttestamentlichen Überlieferungen*, ed. Rolf Rendtorff and Klaus Koch (Neukirchen: Neukirchener Verlag, 1961), pp. 7–32. The phrase is especially important to the tradition of Jeremiah; cf. 1:10; 18:7–10; 24:6; 31:9f.; 42:9f.; 45:4f. On the formula, see Prescott H. Williams, Jr., "Living Toward the Acts of the Savior-Judge," *Austin Seminary Bulletin* 94 (1978): 13–39. That these verbs cluster precisely at the "null-point" in the life of Israel is important for our argument.

40. It is important for our argument that in Israel, God not only brings a word which pulls down and builds up. It is equally important that the word is concretely, historically borne by and entrusted to an identifiable prophet. There is a treasure, but it comes through an "earthen vessel."

41. In the categories of Berger, *Sacred Canopy*, p. 45 and *passim*, we are concerned with the "plausibility structure" of Israel. It is the function of the prophets to criticize and shatter the very "plausibility structure" which the king seeks to uphold in order that God's action may be discerned, even if defined as impossible in the dominant plausibility structure.

42. Ronald E. Clements, "Patterns in the Prophetic Canon," in *Canon and Authority*, ed. George W. Coats and Burke O. Long (Philadelphia: Fortress Press, 1977), pp. 42–55.

43. George Mendenhall, "The Shady Side of Wisdom: The Date and

Purpose of Genesis 3," in *A Light Unto My Path,* ed. H.N. Bream, R.D. Heim, and C.A. Moore (Philadelphia: Temple University Press, 1974), pp. 321–25, has understood this function of the royal class: ". . . the specialist group comes more and more to resemble a primitive tribe whose concern is first to maintain the internal unity, the rigid and secure boundary line against outsiders, and the maintenance of its own power and prestige." See also Glendon Bryce, *A Legacy of Egypt* (Lewisburg, Pa.: Bucknell University Press, 1979), especially chaps. 6–8.

44. Herbert Marcuse, *One-Dimensional Man* (Boston: Beacon Press, 1968), especially chap. 4, speaks of the "suppression of history" by a "closed universe of discourse." When history is suppressed, the past is obliterated and the future is precluded. The present is absolutized either in pride or in despair.

45. On the dynamic relation between the "canon of consensus" and the "canon of disruption," see Susan W. Wittig, "Tradition and Innovation," *Soundings* 61 (1978): 247–59. She contrasts an "aesthetic of conformity" with an "aesthetic of challenge." The latter "is not a comfortable aesthetic, so we can never expect it to be a popular one" (p. 259). In the same issue of *Soundings,* Carol P. Christ, "Heretics and Outsiders," pp. 260–63, speaks of canon and "anti-canon," that is, a literature against the canon of consensus. In some sense this is the function of the prophetic literature of Israel.

46. On hostility to the prophets see Odil H. Steck, *Israel und das gewaltsame Geschick der Propheten,* WMANT 23 (Neukirchen: Neukirchener Verlag, 1967), and less directly Walter Dietrich, *Prophetie and Geschichte,* FRLANT (Gottingen: Vandenhoeck and Ruprecht, 1972). Concerning our theme, their comments refer especially to 2 Kings 17:13–20 and Matt. 5:11–12.

47. On the decisive newness of this particular oracle of judgment, see Ronald Clements, *Prophecy and Covenant,* pp. 39–40. Frank Crüsemann, "Kritik an Amos im deuteronomistischen Geschichtswerk," in *Probleme biblischer Theologie,* ed. Hans Walter Wolff (Munich: Kaiser Verlag, 1971), pp. 57–63, suggests that the critical assertion of Amos is too drastic. So 2 Kings 14:27 is a response which means to refute Amos and to argue that the end is not so inclusive or drastic. The linkage of these two verses perhaps suggests how much the criticism of the prophet is in dispute. Though not directly related to each other, it is also suggestive to relate Amos 8:2, about the end, to Isa. 9:6, which asserts "no end" (*'ên qets*). The claim of Isa. 9:6 is in a royal oracle which reflects precisely the world-view Amos means to penetrate and dismantle.

48. Walther Zimmerli, "Planungen für den Wiederaufbau nach der Katastrophe von 587," in *Studien zur alttestamentlichen Theologie und Pro-*

phetie, TBü 51 (Munich: Kaiser Verlag, 1974), pp. 165–91, writes of "Segen des Nullpunktes" (p. 165), "die Chance des Nullpunktes" (p. 169), and "Gnade des Nullpunktes" (p. 173). See also von Rad, *Old Testament Theology,* vol. 2, pp. 262–77.

49. On the underived character of this proclamation, see Raitt, *Theology of Exile,* pp. 142–52. Raitt is insistent and convincing on this point: ". . . the surprising discovery that *the genre has no 'reason' to explain or justify it.* This means:

There is nothing which provides a logical transition into the announcement of divine intervention.

In human terms, that intervention is not grounded upon anything reasonable.

There is nothing human beings have to do or can do to prepare for this intervention.

The statement of intervention does not lean on any other part of the genre to make sense of it or complete it.

The nature of the communication imprints on abruptness, an unexpectedness, which the prophet let stand.

God's intervention is its own explanation" (p. 145). "The whole thing is God's show! The genre is basically a proclamation of the *intervention* of divine grace. Anything added to that is a footnote" (p. 147). Raitt's argument is primarily a literary one, but it has obvious theological counterparts.

50. "Now, the message of the end of the old and the need to turn to a future act of Yahweh was not itself new—it is also to be found in the eighth-century prophets. With the prophets of our period, however, the gulf between the old and the new has become much wider, the new beginning, which is the future saving event, is much more sharply, and indeed aggressively, marked off from the end of the old," *Old Testament Theology,* vol. 2, p. 271. Von Rad then refers especially to Isa. 43:18; Jer. 23:7, 31:32.

51. On *possibilities* in the gospel that break the *necessities* of life, see Ricoeur, "Language of Faith," pp. 237–38. Prophetic speech thus aims to articulate possibilities that are declared implausible by the plausibility structures of the royal reality. On "impossibilities" in biblical faith, see my article, "'Impossibility' and Epistemology in the Faith Tradition of Abraham and Sarah," to appear in a forthcoming issue of *ZAW.* Special attention is drawn to the double use of "impossible" in Jer. 32:17, 27.

52. Zimmerli, "Prophetic Proclamation," p. 248, raises the issue whether an absolute null point is a possibility or an illusion. No single judgment can be issued on this question because matters are given different nuances in different literary efforts.

53. Although the precise meaning of the phrase is problematic, there is no doubt that it functions in Jeremiah to articulate the unexpected, unexplained emergence of a new possibility for this community which had become hopeless.

54. See a fuller discussion of the term in my paper cited in n. 51.

55. On new claims of authority which lie outside dominant definitions and hope for an alternative reality, see Robert Wilson, *Prophecy and Society in Ancient Israel* (Philadelphia: Fortress Press, 1980). Wilson has argued that much of Israel's prophetic tradition is to be understood as sociologically peripheral and therefore concerned for significant change in social reality. Wilson attends to the sociology of the alternative, but is not much interested in either the epistemological or theological dimensions of the alternative. I suggest that for educational purposes, it is especially the *epistemological* and *theological* dimensions which are important in church education, or education in the "new truth" becomes only one more ideology without staying power.

56. The element of education which concerns us here requires attention to the sociology of knowledge. The title of Jürgen Habermas's book, *Knowledge and Human Interests* (Boston: Beacon Press, 1971), makes the main point. The point is that all *knowledge* is linked to some form of human *interest*. Thus the adherents to "new truth" have not only the problem of establishing some fresh form of authority, but of critiquing the claims of the old revelation which combine theological legitimation and enormous vested interest. It would be a gain in church education simply to nurture people in an awareness of the linkage of knowledge and interest. Not only conventional theology, but also some new psychologies and some new literary theories proceed as if interest has no part in knowledge. The current formal fascination with symbols seems to be based on the conviction that symbols lie prior to and outside the arena of human and vested interest. That is simply a sophisticated form of the argument that God is outside history. Church education needs a heavy dose of a "hermeneutic of suspicion" to counteract such ideological naiveté, for placing the regnant symbols outside a criticism of interest serves unwittingly to absolutize them.

57. This contemporary example has a remarkable parallel to the claims of Joan of Arc who was guided by "voices" which would not submit either to the authority of the crown or the church. George Bernard Shaw has Joan say: "If you command me to declare that all I have done and said, and all the visions and revelations I have had, were not from God, then that is impossible: I would not declare it for anything in the world. What God made me do I will never go back on; and what he has commanded or shall

command I will not fail to do in spite of any man alive. That is what I mean by impossible. And in case the Church should bid me do anything contrary to the command I have from God, I will not consent to it, no matter what it may be." George Bernard Shaw, "Saint Joan," in *Collected Plays VI* (New York: Dodd, Mead and Co., 1973), pp. 173–74. While there is appreciation for her liberating work, there must inevitably be rejection by the *authorities* to which she appeals, for otherwise that would mean the dismantling of established authority. Such a subversive claim is inevitably heretical.

58. The breaking of an accepted rationality and the shattering of a universe of discourse requires speech that stands outside accepted convention. A remarkable discussion of control through controlled language is offered by John M. Cuddihy, *The Ordeal of Civility* (New York: Basic Books, 1974), especially pp. 189–202, in which he shows that *civility* is a more important agenda for some courts than is *justice.* For that reason the prophets of Israel use rhetoric and metaphors that are objectionable and must have violated the sensitivities of many listeners. See most obviously Amos 4:1. A case closer to home: on the very afternoon of writing this note, the antiestablishment candidate for president of the United States, Barry Commoner, is offering a radio commercial for his candidacy. The radio station has apologized profusely that the ad will use the word ("unabbreviated") "bullshit." The station makes clear that it would censor the ad if that were not precluded by the FCC. But no attention is given to the linkage between Commoner's unacceptable *language* and his *unacceptable politics,* both of which endanger conventional definitions of reality and the standard distribution of power. The control of language is important to social control. The prophets of Israel refused an approved language system. When the language is delegitimated, the social realities it constructs are acutely jeopardized. Cuddihy is sensitive to *civility* as the *ritual of socialization* for the status quo. On ritual of control through administrative language, see Marcuse, *One-Dimensional Man.* A prophetic task is to break the control of such linguistic ritual.

59. See the analysis of Phyllis Trible, "The Gift of a Poem," *Andover-Newton Quarterly* 17 (1977): 271–80. Trible's work shows how newness in the world relies on new speech, a claim practiced by Israel's prophets. Her work approaches the practice proposed by Ricoeur.

60. It was Abraham Heschel, *The Prophets* (New York: Harper & Row, 1962), especially chaps. 12–14 and *passim,* who discerned that prophetic grounding is shared suffering in the suffering of God. Since then he has been followed in helpful ways by Kozo Kitamori, *Theology of the Pain of God* (Richmond: John Knox Press, 1965); Jürgen Moltmann, *The Crucified*

God (New York: Harper and Row, 1974), pp. 267–78; and Dorothy Soelle, *Suffering* (Philadelphia: Fortress Press, 1975). But this argument need not be made only on biblical and theological grounds. It can also be made on experiential grounds. On the major questions before our society, there is a strange alliance between *pain* and *truth*. It is the experience of pain which brings discernment about the truth. Those who offer truth without experiencing the pain are likely not to be trusted. I submit that this reality among us responds to the main claims of a theology of the cross.

61. Much of this was anticipated by H. Wheeler Robinson in his three important but neglected books, *The Cross in the Old Testament* (Philadelphia: Westminster Press, 1955), *The Cross of Hosea* (Philadelphia: Westminster Press, 1949), and *The Cross of Jeremiah* (London: SCM, 1925).

62. Hermann Gunkel, *Genesis*, 2nd ed., HAT (Göttingen: Vandenhoeck and Ruprecht, 1902), p. 27. The phrase is, "der Vernunft ohne Pathos."

CHAPTER 4

1. See Brevard S. Childs, *Introduction to the Old Testament as Scripture* (Philadelphia: Fortress Press, 1979), pp. 65–67.

2. The phrase is not easy to interpret. James Crenshaw, *Prophetic Conflict*, BZAW 124 (Berlin: Walter de Gruyter, 1971), pp. 116–23, has presented a useful summary of the problem. I am, however, not convinced by his conclusion: "In short, between Thus said the Lord, and Listen, my son, to your father's advice, there is no fundamental difference" (p. 123). It is not disputed that wisdom teaching also has a theological source. But it does not follow that the claims for authority are the same among wisdom teachers as prophets. Crenshaw restates the matter in "Wisdom," in *Old Testament Form Criticism*, ed. John H. Hayes (San Antonio: Trinity University Press, 1974), pp. 229–39.

3. The argument of Norman Whybray is in the direction of an intellectual option, as is evident from the title of his book, *The Intellectual Tradition in the Old Testament*, BZAW 135 (New York: Walter de Gruyter, 1974).

4. Gerhard von Rad, *Wisdom in Israel* (New York: Abingdon, 1972), chap. 4, is especially eloquent on this matter.

5. A summary of recent scholarly developments in the field will be well summarized by Crenshaw in his new introduction to wisdom, *Old Testament Wisdom: An Introduction* (Atlanta: John Knox Press, 1981).

6. We have not yet appropriated for education the resources available in these materials. Mention should be made of the discussion of Richard Banzhaf, "Proverbs, Ecclesiastes and Modern Religious Education," *Religion in Life* 37 (1968): 364–81, and to two papers by Charles Melchert, including "Wisdom on Old-New Paradigm for Education" (unpublished

1974) and "The Sage as Paradigm for the Religious Educator," *Living Light* 16 (1979): 79–89.

7. See especially Erhard Gerstenberger, *Wesen und Herkunft des "Apodikischen Rechts,"* WMANT 20 (Neukirchen: Neukirchener Verlag, 1965). In relation to that seminal work, see Hans Walter Wolff, *Amos the Prophet* (Philadelphia: Fortress Press, 1973). Wolff's book was published in German before Gerstenberger's, but the two are closely linked and likely mutually informed.

8. That is, this teaching held together practicality and morality. Von Rad, *Wisdom in Israel,* pp. 60–63, observes how the wisdom teachers did not choose between the experience of the world and the experience of God: "Rather, we see the teachers—with what sometimes appears to us as an uncanny confidence—holding together the awareness of inherent determination on the one hand and faith in Yahweh's power on the other, indeed even mingling the two" (p. 60).

9. On the linkage of morality and conformity, see Walter Brueggemann, "A Neglected Sapiential Word Pair," *ZAW* 89 (1977): 234–58. Integrity and perversion are understood in terms of the moral and practical norms of the community. The "good" is what is conventionally approved in the community. See also Bennett, "Wisdom Motifs in Psalm 14—15—nābāt and 'iṣāh," BASOR 220 (1975), pp. 15–21.

10. Peter Berger and Thomas Luckmann, *The Social Construction of Reality* (Garden City, N.Y.: Doubleday, 1966), pp. 92–104. For our purposes, it is instructive that they cite proverbs and moral maxims as a system of legitimation for a social order (p. 94).

11. The configuration of such teachings becomes a life-world for the young. Gerstenberger, *Wesen und Herkunft,* p. 50, has suggested that Prov. 3:7 is a "motto" and epitome of this clan socialization:

Be not wise in your own eyes;

fear the Lord, and turn away from evil.

The first line submits the individual learner to the teaching of the community. The second line balances the key affirmation with the most decisive prohibition. The saying offers a context for concreteness, but already the main claims of authority and legitimation are established.

12. The argument has been most forcefully put by Hans-Jürgen Hermisson, *Studien zur israelitischen Spruchweisheit,* WMANT 28 (Neukirchen: Neukirchener Verlag, 1968). Von Rad, *Wisdom,* chap. 2, is inclined in this direction as well, but with appropriate caution. See also his positive but restrained comments about the hypothesis of clan wisdom, pp. 11–12.

13. Note the reference of William McKane, *Proverbs,* The Old Testament Library (Philadelphia: Westminster Press, 1970), p. 301, to Machia-

vellian rule and preferred alternatives. Such a comment brings the text close to the realities of courtly power.

14. This form is especially important for both court and clan wisdom. Gerstenberger links it especially to the "father-teacher" in the clan, tribe, or didactic community. See the treatment of McKane, *Proverbs,* pp. 10–22, though his categories are quite complicated. The form-critical matters have been well summarized by Crenshaw, "Wisdom," pp. 229–39.

15. This form is expressed with many variations and is variously referred to in the scholarly literature as "Sentence," "Mashal." Cf. McKane, *Proverbs,* pp. 22–23; von Rad, *Wisdom,* pp. 25–34.

16. Crenshaw, "Wisdom," p. 235, challenges such a judgment, but I see no compelling evidence against the notion of "self-validation."

17. Ibid., p. 236, rightly warns against drawing too close a connection between any particular *form* and any proposed *setting*: "The absence of any correspondence in wisdom literature between form and setting renders a decision between these virtually impossible: a further complication is the fact that the prehistory of the legal admonition is the everyday intercourse of human activity. In addition, there is in court wisdom an intermingling of agricultural imagery and other concerns of the *Sippenethos* with the more office-oriented interests of the *Gruppenethos*. It is thus not possible to limit agricultural metaphors to folk wisdom, royal concerns to court wisdom; accordingly, the precise origin of any passage is open to question." Thus consideration of both clan and court wisdom remains in the realm of hypotheses for which we do not have decisive data. Nonetheless, the hypotheses serve to raise issues about authority and the sociology of value.

18. Whybray, *Intellectual Tradition.*

19. See the brief but discerning characterization of the chapter by von Rad, *Wisdom,* pp. 145–49.

20. Von Rad, *Wisdom,* has commented convincingly on the orderliness of life, which can be discerned: Wisdom expresses "faith in the similarity of men and of their reactions, faith in the reliability of the orders which support human life and thus, implicitly or explicitly, faith in God who put these orders into operation" (pp. 62–63). "The *saddiq* is a man who, as we also sometimes express it, is 'in order'" (p. 79). "The man who is without honor is the fool (Prov. 26:1, 8), the 'disorderly' man who, possibly from inner weakness, is unable to adapt himself to that order which is imposed on all men." (p. 83). "This social order is regarded as given and is obviously stable" (p. 85). See also his earlier discussion, *Old Testament Theology,* vol. 1 (New York: Harper and Brothers, 1962), pp. 418–41. "Empirical and gnomic wisdom starts from the unyielding presupposition that there is a hidden order in things and events—only, it has to be dis-

cerned in them, with great patience and at the cost of all kinds of painful experience. And this order is kindly and righteous" (p. 421). Von Rad has addressed primarily the question of the *experience* of this order. The other part of this general argument is well articulated by H. H. Schmidt, *Gerechtigkeit als Weltordnung* (Tübingen: J.C. B. Mohr, Paul Siebeck, 1968), who stresses the cosmic, ontological aspect of this order. But there is no tension between these claims. The assumption of wisdom is precisely the convergence of these two insights: (1) there is a reliable order to reality, and (2) it is given to us in daily experience for those capable of discernment. In his paper, "The World-View of Biblical Proverbs," (unpublished, 1978), Brian W. Kovacs has shown how the wisdom tradition reflects on the coherence of life without reducing that coherence to fixity or rigidity. It is that coherence without fixity that made wisdom reflection open to new data and given to a rich variety of articulation: ". . . it should be becoming increasingly apparent that these wise lived in a polyvalent universe. They interpreted and valued their experience in terms of a number of different, sometimes conflicting goods" (p. 7). On the discernment of order as the center of education, see Gregory Bateson, *Steps to an Ecology of the Mind* (New York: Ballantine, 1975), p. xxiii and *passim*.

21. See Peter Berger, *Sacred Canopy* (Garden City, N.Y.: Doubleday, 1967), p. 53. He comments on "the recurrent intrusion into individual and collective experience of the anomic (or, if one prefers, denomizing) phenomena of suffering, evil, and above all, death . . . The anomic phenomena must not only be lived through, they must also be explained—to wit, explained in terms of the nomos established in the society in question." Our argument here thus appeals to a convergence of (1) the structure of the poem of Job which pivots on Job 28, (2) von Rad's insight into proverbial wisdom in terms of order, and (3) Berger's insight concerning nomos and anomie in a sociology of theodicy.

22. The dialogue is an unequal one not only because the teacher has more experience, but because the teacher also has all the social power of legitimated authority, that is, the weight of traditional teaching not only may square with authority, but "because we say so."

23. On the basis of science in such amazement before the coherence of the world, see Michael Polanyi, *The Tacit Dimension* (Garden City, N.Y.: Doubleday Anchor Books, 1966), p. 70: "My assertion that science can have discipline and originality only if it believes that the facts and values bear on a still unrevealed reality, stands in opposition to the current philosophic conception of scientific knowledge." More recently, see the discerning and comprehensive statement of A. R. Peacocke, *Creation and the World of Science* (Oxford: Clarendon Press, 1979), and Harold K. Schilling,

The Consciousness in Science and Religion (Philadelphia: United Church Press, 1973).

24. My argument, then, is that there is a match between the literary placement of Job 28 and the move in epistemology which it serves. In its backward look there is a correlation: (1) the poem as *literature* looks back to the settledness of the prologue and the epistemological certitude of Job and his friends; and (2) the poem as *epistemological revolution* looks back to a mode of knowledge which was confident and free of every self doubt. Conversely the look forward also offers the same match: (1) the poem as *literature* looks forward to the final challenge of Job (31) and the massive overriding character of the whirlwind, all of which serves to displace all of Job's certitude and even his capacity for self-assertion; and (2) the poem as *epistemological revolution* looks forward to terror and brooding, to not knowing and being led into an intellectual world where the old *nomos* of Israel is in crisis. Literarily, the poem thus means to lead Israel into and through that crisis. The literature is itself a facet of the redefinition of Israel's knowledge. Von Rad, *Wisdom*, p. 4, comments on the connection between the experience and the linguistic expression of it. While affirming his insight, I would assign a more crucial role to language and literature, not only to give *expression* to the experience, but to *evoke the experience* and perhaps to be the very experience. Thus Job 28 leads Israel into and through the experiential crisis.

25. Job's friends wanted to reduce knowledge of the mystery of life to *usability.* And indeed, so did Job. That is, if one knows the mysteries, one can harness the powers for one's well-being. There is not much difference between that old moralism which claims to know the mind of God and the new forms of technical knowledge which seek to manipulate "nature" by knowing more. Both forms of technical knowledge deny the mystery. In the old forms of moralism, genuine faith becomes impossible. In the new forms of technical knowledge, genuine science becomes impossible.

26. Von Rad, *Wisdom*, p. 73, quotes Guardini who refers to "the mystery in what is utterly clear." Note the implication of how I have postured *looking back* and *looking forward.* The argument is the inverse of the usual assumption of modernity. It is assumed that we look back to old traditions and old mysteries, but as we penetrate the mysteries and move out of the traditions, we move forward to new knowledge, new freedom, and new power. The argument of Job is in the opposite direction. Human capacity for management is where we are coming from, and into the deeper secret of God is where we are headed. This is a critical challenge to every Enlightenment notion of progress. Such an argument in the structure of the poem of Job, of course, can only be made at a certain moment in the life of society.

But I submit that in our society we may be at just such a moment when we discover that things are reversed. What we thought was progress in emancipation may be looking backward, and what we thought were old divine mysteries may indeed be looking forward.

27. Ibid., pp. 63–64.

28. See the summaries of Crenshaw already cited, and von Rad, *Wisdom*, chap. 3.

29. The linkage between deed and consequence is undoubtedly one of the major assumptions of wisdom teaching, even if that tradition has no monopoly on it. See the summary of von Rad, *Wisdom*, pp. 128–37. This teaching has two very different aspects to it. First, it is firm and undoubted that things have such a connection. This is doubted only in Ecclesiastes, with hints in Job; only Job refuses that alternative. But second, the linkage between "sowing and reaping" is not transparent. A great deal of data is needed as well as careful reflection. A great deal of moral education needs to be undertaken about the practice of making linkages between deed and consequence. That education faces two fronts. On the one hand, many of our old assumptions about this no longer hold. On the other hand, there is therefore a temptation to conclude that there are no such inevitable links. The wisdom teachers rejected both of these conclusions for the harder work of continuing discernment.

30. See Glendon E. Bryce, "'Better'-Proverbs: An Historical and Structural Study," Proceedings of the Society of Biblical Literature II (1972), pp. 343–54, and Graham S. Ogden, "The 'Better'-Proverb (Tob-Spruch), Rhetorical Criticism and Qoheleth," *JBL* 96 (1977): 498–505.

31. Von Rad, *Wisdom*, pp. 38–40.

32. Cf. John Priest, "Humanism, Skepticism, and Pessimism in Israel," *JAAR* 34 (1968): 311–26.

33. On this Psalm, James L. Mays, "What is Man . . .?" in *From Faith to Faith*, ed. Dikran Y. Hadidian (Pittsburgh: Pickwick Press, 1979), pp. 203–81, shows how such an anthropocentric statement must be rooted in a confession of God.

34. See my summary of these dimensions of wisdom in *In Man We Trust* (Richmond: John Knox Press, 1972).

35. George Mendenhall, "The Shady Side of Wisdom: The Date and Purpose of Genesis 3," in *A Light Unto My Path*, ed. Howard N. Bream, Ralph D. Heim, and Carey A. Moore (Philadelphia: Temple University Press, 1974), pp. 319–34.

36. It is no longer possible to sustain the old notion of development from utilitarian to theological wisdom. McKane, *Proverbs*, pp. 11 and 415, by his literary classification, appears still to hold such a view. But that long-

held notion must be abandoned, especially in light of the work of von Rad. The latter has made clear that even the most "primitive" wisdom teaching is already theologically aware.

37. To my knowledge, we do not have an adequate study of "plan" as an element of wisdom instruction. Von Rad, "The Joseph Narrative," in *The Problem of the Hexateuch and Other Essays* (New York: McGraw-Hill, 1966), pp. 296–300, and *Genesis*, The Old Testament Library (Philadelphia: Westminster Press, 1972), pp. 438–40, has recognized the problem and possibility, but has not pursued it. J. William Whedbee, *Isaiah and Wisdom* (Nashville: Abingdon Press, 1971), pp. 114–26, follows von Rad with illuminating comments. But his focus is not on the term "plan," which occurs in Gen. 50:20. Bertel Albrektson, *History and the Gods* (Lund: Gleerup, 1967), chap. 5, has suggested that "plan" is not peculiarly appropriate to the Old Testament tradition. His attention is on the "historical" traditions. I suggest Israelite wisdom shares with other wisdom the notion of a "plan." But perhaps in Israel it is more insistently a theonomous plan.

38. On "providence," see the shrewd comments of Karl Barth, *Church Dogmatics*, vol. 3, ed. G.W. Bromiley and T.F. Torrance (Edinburgh: T. & T. Clark, Ltd., 1960), pp. 3, 35. In Genesis 22, the text has the strange use of *ra'ah*, commonly meaning "see," but here conventionally rendered "provide." Barth handles this odd tradition of translation by a play on words "video," "pro-video"; thus "to provide" is to see ahead of time what is needed. It is then a simple move from *provide* to *providence*. And indeed, the wisdom teachers present God as the one who sees ahead what will be needed by creation.

39. Von Rad, *Old Testament Theology*, vol. 1, pp. 418–41, has offered the most discerning discussion of this matter. See especially the texts to which he refers on p. 439. See the derivative discussion of Whedbee, *Isaiah and Wisdom*, pp. 117–26.

40. Von Rad, *Genesis*, p. 434, observes how these issues are at the root of the "undertone of despair" and skepticism which surfaces in Eccles. 3:11; 7:25; 8:17; 11:5. That is, the problems articulated in Ecclesiastes are not new questions, but are old and deep in the awarenesses of the wisdom teachers.

41. In commenting on Gen. 50:20, von Rad, "The Joseph Narrative," p. 297, writes: "Thus the statements of what 'you meant' and what 'God meant' are in the last analysis irreconcilable." It is the irreconcilable set of assertions which is the problem of wisdom. But it is also the task of wisdom to sort this out as best it can be done. That same issue is well put in Prov. 25:2–3, where wisdom is the relation of concealing and finding out.

42. The matter of "limit" has been best put by Walther Zimmerli, "The Place and Limit of the Wisdom in the Framework of the Old Testament Theology," reprinted in *Studies in Ancient Israelite Wisdom*, ed. James L. Crenshaw (New York: KTAV, 1976), pp. 314–26.

43. Again it is von Rad who has put the matter so shrewdly. He writes in *God at Work in Israel* (Nashville: Abingdon Press, 1980), p. 180: "When we talk about experiencing limits, we tend today to think primarily negatively, to see something that interrupts human activity. But when the ancients put their minds to understand the mystery that lies between human planning and the actual realization of those plans, and when they saw there a particular field for God's providence, then these limits appeared in a different light. Were they not to be considered as something beneficial? Could there not, equally well, be seen in that which man feels is a limit God's providential care which guards man against his own follies and does not abandon him to his human wisdom about limits? Knowledge about the divine presence in all human activity, now setting a limit to man's plans, now carrying them far beyond the stated goal, was ultimately comforting." In his comments on Prov. 21:30–31, von Rad says: "In this astonishing maxim, knowledge about limits is formulated in an especially radical way. The maxim becomes particularly astonishing when one realizes that it does not intend to admonish man about the acquisition and use of wisdom. Its intention was only to guard against the error that there is a guarantee for success in mustering the most superior human wisdom. A person must always remain ready for the act of God that is completely excluded from every reckoning. There is always a great unknown between the mustering of the most reliable wisdom and what then finally happens: it is a gulf which the most realistic knowledge of life is unable to bridge."

44. See the discussion of this passage by Glendon Bryce, *The Legacy of Egypt* (Lewisburg, Pa.: Bucknell University Press, 1979), pp. 142–62. Bryce has gone beyond normal historical analysis to make some shrewd sociological comments.

45. See *Old Testament Theology*, vol. 1, pp. 418–41, and *Wisdom*, especially chaps. 4 and 5.

46. On *discernment* and *interconnectedness*, James Carroll, *A Terrible Beauty* (New York: Newman Press, 1973), pp. 39–40, writes: "How do the rich, the powerful, the easy of us see with the eyes of the poor on whose possessions we trample, of the hungry on whose last ewe lamb we feed? It is a matter of *seeing connections*, what we have been calling conversion. See the connection between yourself and the other . . . Seeing! Conversion is a matter of *seeing*" (italics in the original).

47. On the connections of healing and placebo, see Norman Cousins,

Anatomy of an Illness (New York: W. W. Norton and Co., 1979), chap. 2.

48. Peter Berger, *The Homeless Mind* (New York: Random House, Vintage Books, 1973). His word for the process of treating life in discrete units or "packages" is "componentiality."

49. An example of the capacity of modernity to bracket out some segments of life, as if they can be isolated, is evident in the testimony of FBI agent Sullivan concerning FBI treatment of Martin Luther King, Jr. Sullivan testified: "Never once did I hear anybody, including myself, raise the question, is this course of action which we have agreed upon lawful, . . . is it ethical or moral? We never gave any thought to this realm of reasoning, because we were just naturally pragmatists. The one thing we were concerned about [was] will this course of action work, will it get us what we want . . . ? I think this suggests really in government we are amoral." Quoted by Harris Wofford, *Of Kennedys and Kings* (New York: Farrar, Strauss, and Giroux, 1980), p. 220. The assumption is that this piece of a pragmatic agenda can be isolated from other dimensions of society.

50. Roland Murphy, "Qoheleth's 'Quarrel' with the Fathers," in *From Faith to Faith*, ed. Dikran Y. Hadidian (Pittsburgh: Pickwick Press, 1979), pp. 235–45, has offered a discerning comment about the dynamic of the wisdom tradition. Specifically, he sees that the writers (and final editor) of Ecclesiastes are not iconoclasts who reject the wisdom tradition, but they themselves are practitioners of wisdom teaching. While they challenge the specific conclusions of their predecessors, they themselves are utilizing the same perspectives to make their own contribution to the ongoing task. Thus even in this late and radical literature, the perspective and task is unchanged. Even there the teachers cling to their conviction about the hiddenness and reality of the connections. The "quarrel" is in the family.

51. The wisdom tradition always works at the interaction between *new data* that comes out of experience and *abiding convictions* that precede the data but are always reformulated in light of the data. I suggest that in Job and even more in Ecclesiastes, there is a sense of the failure of the data to show the interrelatedness that must be there. But even this gap between data and conviction does not lead to an abandonment of the conviction. One may suggest that the biblical resolution is to cling to this conviction in any case. Conversely, the modern resolution is to give up any such conviction and to hold to the data, though in "packages" and "time-frames" which are from time to time "inoperative" and "operative." The disjunction between *data* and *conviction* leads to the question of theodicy. Thus Berger, *Sacred Canopy*, chap. 3, probes the rise of theodicy in relation to the sociology of knowledge. It is not without reason that the so-called "question of theodicy" in the Old Testament comes precisely in the wisdom teachers, who struggle with the relation of *data* and *conviction*. See the

judicious comments on wisdom and theodicy by James Crenshaw, ed., *Studies in Ancient Israelite Wisdom*, pp. 26–35. See also Crenshaw's more specific statement, "The Problem of Theodicy in Sirach," *JBL* 94 (1975): 47–64.

52. The phrase is Klaus Koch's. See the summary of von Rad, *Wisdom*, pp. 128–37.

53. If I rightly understand the closely reasoned proposal of Gerald T. Sheppard, *Wisdom as a Hermeneutical Construct*, BZAW 151 (Berlin: Walter de Gruyter, 1980), his argument concerns the way in which wisdom serves to keep the Torah alive and pertinent to the ongoing reflection of Israel. That is, all of Israel's literature (including the Torah) is now filtered through the perspectives of the wisdom teachers. See especially pp. 12–18, 116–19. See also Sheppard's statement, "Hearing the Voice of the Same God through Historically Dissimilar Traditions," *Interpretation* 36 (1982): 21–33.

54. See particularly the presentation of von Rad, *Wisdom*, pp. 144–49.

55. Glendon Bryce, "'Better'-Proverbs," p. 207, commenting on the canon of the Old Testament, says that the Torah and prophets present *Deus revelatus*, whereas wisdom presents *Deus absconditus*. That is the argument of von Rad's recent book, *God at Work in Israel*. This is a most remarkable recognition, precisely because the wisdom teachers seem to want to make things clear and evident. But that is also the playfulness of their teaching, that as things become *evident*, they become at bottom all the more *inscrutable*. That is the interplay of hidden and evident which concerns education in this tradition. Such education is urgent in a context of modernity because technical knowledge tends to know everything shamelessly and one-dimensionally. The wisdom teachers see the inscrutable character of that which is most evident to us.

56. The verse is rejected in the careful study of Carol Woodson Bernard, "The Hymn to Wisdom: Exegesis of Job 28:20–28," *Duke Divinity School Review* 39 (1974): 117; see von Rad, *Wisdom*, pp. 148–49. Marvin Pope, *Job*, Anchor Bible 15 (Garden City, N.Y.: Doubleday, 1965), p. 183, also offers the usual judgments against the verse. On the other hand, the verse is not without its defenders. Cf., for example, Artur Weiser, *Das Buch Hiob* (Göttingen: Vandenhoeck and Ruprecht, 1959), p. 200, for a contrary opinion. See also Harmut Gese, *Zur biblische Theologie* (Munich: Kaiser Verlag, 1977), pp. 71–74. The function of the verse, however, cannot be decided on its "fit" into the coherence of chapter 28. Indeed, its placement here, whether original or not, is crucial for the present claims of the text. I conclude the verse is not "an antidote to the agnostic tenor of the preceding poem" (Pope), but rather is the conclusion the wisdom teachers necessarily draw from the flow of the poem. That is, wisdom is retained to God.

What humankind knows is enough for obedience, and that is expressed as "fear of God."

57. E. Gerstenberger, *Wesen und Herkunft*, p. 49, takes Prov. 3:7 as a summary of Proverbs. Our argument suggests that in Job 28:28 the boldest wisdom teachers are unable to advance beyond that same statement.

58. Pope, *Job*, observes that the form of "lord" here *('dny)* is not the same as the familiar expression in Proverbs and occurs nowhere else in Job. Thus the conventional English translation may suggest a closer parallel than in fact exists.

CHAPTER 5

1. The literature is summarized in the following studies: Erhard Gerstenberger, "Psalms," in *Old Testament Form Criticism*, ed. John H. Hayes (San Antonio: Trinity University Press, 1974), pp. 179–223; John H. Hayes, *An Introduction to Old Testament Study* (Nashville: Abingdon Press, 1979), pp. 285–317; Ronald Clements, *One Hundred Years of Old Testament Interpretation* (Philadelphia: Westminster Press, 1976), pp. 76–98. Reference should still be made to the older summary of Aubrey Johnson, "The Psalms," in *The Old Testament and Modern Study*, ed. H. H. Rowley (Oxford: Clarendon Press, 1951), pp. 167–209. Most recently, see the assessment of J. H. Eaton, "The Psalms and Israelite Worship," in *Tradition and Interpretation*, ed. G. W. Anderson (Oxford: Clarendon Press, 1979), pp. 238–73.

2. Claus Westermann, *The Praise of God in the Psalms* (Richmond: John Knox Press, 1965). See also the more comprehensive summary of Westermann, *The Psalms: Structure, Content and Message* (Minneapolis: Augsburg, 1980).

3. It is structurally important to the Old Testament theology of Gerhard von Rad that Psalms figure as Israel's *answer* to the God of the Torah tradition. See *Old Testament Theology*, vol. 1 (New York: Harper and Row, 1962), pp. 354–418.

4. By "convenantal," of course, I do not refer either to the Hittite treaty hypothesis of Mendenhall or to the imperial paradigm of Eichrodt. Rather, I refer to the more elemental presupposition of the Bible that Yahweh and Israel have decisively to do with each other. See my general use of "covenant" in this sense in "Covenanting as Human Vocation," *Interpretation* 33 (1979): 115–29, and my article, "Covenant as Subversive Paradigm," *Christian Century* 97 (1980): 1094–99.

5. Paul Ricoeur especially has pursued this question in relation to biblical faith. On the gains from Ricoeur, see the convenient review of John Dominic Crossan, *Cliffs of Fall* (New York: Seabury Press, 1980), especially chap. 1.

6. By this I mean that if Israel's relation to God is uniformly humble, submissive, and self-depreciating, this serves as a model for docility in all of life, that is, as acceptance of all established authority. On the other hand, if there is boldness, risk, and assertion on Israel's part toward God, this becomes a model of self-assertiveness in the face of every authority, human as well as divine. This latter mode of worship is, of course, indispensable for a genuine practice of liberation. On the interplay of *submission* and *protest* in relation to God in the Psalms, see Claus Westermann, "The Role of Lament in the Theology of the Old Testament," *Interpretation* 28 (1974): 20–38. The submissiveness of much Christian worship models docility of a stoic kind rather than the *hutzpah* of Psalmic prayer.

7. The language of the overwhelming and inescapable meeting with God is articulated in Amos 9:2–4, which is closely linked to the Psalmic tradition of Ps. 139:7–12. See Hans-Joachim Kraus, *Theologie der Psalmen* (Neukirchen: Neukirchener Verlag, 1979), pp. 184–85. The "Thou" is accessible but hidden. In his comments on Psalm 73, Samuel Terrien, *The Elusive Presence* (New York: Harper and Row, 1978), pp. 316–17, writes: "An inquisitive essay has become a prayer. The skeptic, who pondered intellectual answers to difficult questions, suddenly addressed the Deity As "Thou." He inserted his doubt into the context of his adoration . . . At the very core of his *Anfechtung*, the thinker found out that his cosmic solitude was an illusion. He was not alone. All along, though without knowing it, he had been in the immediate company of Yahweh. Perhaps he stressed the *I-with-Thee* formula (vvs. 32b, 23a, 25a) to show that his egocentric endeavor had been unwittingly oriented Godward. In any case, he was now raised to a new level of knowledge." In his last book, *God at Work in Israel* (Nashville: Abingdon Press, 1980), von Rad broods over the hiddenness of God and the inscrutability of life which leads to resignation. In his study of Psalm 90, p. 217, he writes: "The resignation, however, was too burdensome. Let us say it calmly: God was too far from that realm of dark and bitter reflection, in which the psalm was moving, to be addressed. Now, however, the spell is broken; the psalm has at last found again the divine 'thou,' and there is scarcely a halt to the petitions." The finding of the divine "Thou" is an urgent possibility in church education. It has to do with attentiveness to a language which our culture finds either absurd or subversive.

8. Rainer Albertz, *Persönliche Frömmigkeit and offizielle Religion,* Calwer Theologische Monographien A, 9 (Stuttgart: Calwer Verlag, 1978), pp. 48, 87, and *passim,* indicates the history of intimacy which stands behind and is reflected in much of the Psalter.

9. See my fuller statement of this in *Praying the Psalms* (Winona, Minn.: St. Mary's Press, 1982). I have argued that it is the intense Jewish-

ness of the Psalter which makes the Psalms most problematic and most urgent for us,

10. Recall again George Santayana's comment on religious particularity: "Any attempt to speak without speaking any particular language is not more hopeless than the attempt to have a religion that shall be no religion in particular . . . Thus every living and healthy religion has a marked idiosyncrasy. Its power consists in its special and surprising message and in the bias which that revelation gives to life. The vistas it opens and the mysteries it propounds are another world to live in; and another world to live in—whether we expect ever to pass wholly over into it or not—is what we mean by having a religion." From Santayana's *Reason in Religion*, quoted by Clifford Geertz, "Religion as a Cultural System," in *Anthropological Approaches to the Study of Religion*, ed. Michael Banton (London: Tavistock Publications, 1966).

11. Karl Barth, *Protestant Theology in the Nineteenth Century* (Valley Forge: Judson Press, 1978) pp. 33-173.

12. The catechetical tradition has asserted this consistently. *The Heidelberg Catechism* in its first question and answer says it so eloquently and simply: "What is your only comfort, in life and in death? That I belong—body and soul, in life and in death—not to myself, but to my faithful Savior, Jesus Christ. . . ." *The Heidelberg Catechism* (Philadelphia: United Church Press, 1962), p. 9. The *Evangelical Catechism* (St. Louis: Eden Publishing House, 1961), p. 75, concludes with a parallel affirmation of grounding in this "Thou": "Lord Jesus, for thee I live, for thee I suffer, for thee I die! Lord Jesus, thine will I be in life and death! Grant me, O Lord, eternal salvation! Amen." Now it happens that both examples are christological. But that is not my point. The point is rather that genuine biblical faith is addressed to a concrete identifiable "Thou," whose name we know. The language can as well address the God of Israel as the Lord of the church.

13. Martin Buber, *I and Thou* (New York: Charles Scribner and Sons, 1955). See Daniel S. Breslauer, *The Chrysalis of Religion* (Nashville: Abingdon Press, 1980) for the Jewish roots and context of Buber's "I-Thou."

14. Artur Weiser, *The Psalms*, Old Testament Library (Philadelphia: Westminster Press, 1962), pp. 531-32, has seen that the Psalm turns on v. 10, which is the turning point between the lament which precedes and the hymn which follows. But it is not only a move from lament to hymn. It is a move from "I" to "Thou." "The form of the verse and its position between lament and hymn also expresses the importance inasmuch as the worshipper here realizes and confesses that the way described in his lament

is the wrong way which in the end always leads him only to his own self and to his affliction, but never enables him to come into contact with God by faith." See Weiser's critical study, "Psalm 77. Ein Beitrag zur Frage nach dem Verhaltnis von Kult and Heilsgeschichte," *ThLZ* 72 (1947): 133–40.

15. See the discussion by James F. Ross, "Psalm 73," in *Israelite Wisdom*, ed. John G. Gammie et al. (Missoula, Mont.: Scholars Press, 1978), pp. 161–75. See also Walther Zimmerli, *Man and his Hope in the Old Testament*, SBT 20 (Naperville: Alec R. Allenson, n.d.), pp. 40–41, *Old Testament Theology in Outline* (Atlanta: John Knox Press, 1978), p. 165, and Gerhard von Rad, *Old Testament Theology*, vol. 1 (New York: Harper and Row, 1965), pp. 405–7. Both von Rad and Zimmerli see that the crucial resource of the Psalm is the capacity to confess that "Yahweh is my portion," which frees from anxiety for every other portion. But that confession depends upon the reality of the "Thou" who is addressed. Address to that "Thou" turns the structure of the Psalm even as it turns the life of the speaker.

16. Self-groundedness occurs when God becomes an *object* to be discussed and analyzed rather than the *subject* to be addressed in complaint and praise. Dietrich Bonhoeffer, *Creation and Fall* (New York: Macmillan Co., 1959), pp. 69–72, has characterized the serpent of Genesis 3 as devising a "religious question," for that was the first one who talked *about* God rather than *addressing God*. It is that distance which leads to narcissistic self-groundedness. As we shall see in our final discussion, the problem of *nearness and distance* concerned not only the Psalmists but also the teachers of Deuteronomy. See Brevard S. Childs, *Myth and Reality in the Old Testament*, *SBT* 27 (Naperville: Alec R. Allenson, 1960), pp. 43–47.

17. Martin Buber, *Tales of the Hasadim, The Early Masters* (New York: Schocken Books, 1947), p. 212. See also Buber's discussion of Psalm 73 in *Right and Wrong* (London: SCM Press, 1952), pp. 34–52. In the latter, Buber (pp. 44–45) notes that this Psalmist no longer says, "Thou art with me," as in Ps. 23:5, but now "I am continually with thee." The relationship has been inverted. Clearly "who is with whom" asserts a great deal about the character of faith and spirituality.

18. John H. Westerhoff, *Will Our Children Have Faith?* (New York: Seabury, 1976).

19. All three uses of *baṭaḥ* in this Psalm are linked to fear:

When I *fear*—I put my *trust* in thee . . . (v. 3)

I will not *fear*—I *trust* in God . . . (v. 4)

I will not *fear*—I *trust* in God . . . (v.11).

See also Ps. 27:1–3:

whom shall I *fear* . . .
my heart will not *fear*
. . . yet I will be *confident (baṭaḥ)*.

20. Erik H. Erikson, *Identity and the Life Cycle* (New York: International University Press, Inc., 1959), pp. 55–65.

21. The Hebrew has a double use of *baṭaḥ* here:
What do you *trust* this *trust?*

22. These texts are notoriously difficult at every level. See the comment of Brevard S. Childs, *Isaiah and the Assyrian Crisis,* SBT 3 (Naperville: Alec R. Allenson, 1967), p. 85, on the term *baṭaḥ* in the traditioning process of these narratives. Now on the theological issues in the text, see also Ronald Clements, *Isaiah and the Deliverance of Jerusalem, JSOT* Sup. 13 (Sheffield: University Press, 1980).

23. On "Yahweh is my portion," see Gerhard von Rad, "'Righteousness' and 'Life' in the Cultic Language of the Psalms," *The Problem of the Hextateuch and Other Essays* (New York: McGraw-Hill, 1966), pp. 253–66, and Zimmerli, *Old Testament Theology in Outline*, pp. 93–99. Von Rad argues in a spiritualizing direction. Such a spiritualizing need not move toward social docility, but can result in new energy for concrete hope.

24. The full verse of the gospel hymn is:
When we walk with the Lord in the Sight of his Word
What a glory He sheds on our Way!
While we do his good will, he abides with us still,
And with all who will trust and obey.
Trust and obey, for there is no other way,
To be happy in Jesus, but to trust and obey.
On the same theme Jon Sobrino, *Christology at the Crossroads: A Latin American Approach,* trans. John Drury (Maryknoll, N.Y.: Orbis Books, 1978), p. 106, has this pertinent comment: "Jesus does not reveal the absolute mystery of God. He reveals how one may respond to that absolute mystery through *trust and obedience* to the mission of the Kingdom" (italics added).

25. Abraham Heschel, *Who is Man?* (Stanford: University Press, 1965), p. 97.

26. Ibid., p. 111.

27. John Calvin, *Institutes of the Christian Religion,* Library of Christian Classics 20 (Philadelphia: Westminster Press, 1960) I, 6, 2, p. 72. See the comments by Charles M. Wood, "The Knowledge Born of Obedience," *ATR* 61 (1979): 331–40. Wood addresses the problem we inherit from the Enlightenment, which is suspicious of any dependence that knowledge has on obedience. He argues that in important ways Calvin would agree with

Kant that obedience does not require renunciation of the freedom of thought: "One does not come to a right knowledge of God, in Calvin's view, by taking someone's word for it. One comes to know God by actually *doing* something, i.e., by obeying. Obedience is not a substitute for knowledge, nor a way of getting over one's desire for knowledge, nor a way of convincing oneself of something. It is, simply a way to knowledge; it is the route by which one may come to one's knowledge of God. At least, that is what Calvin seems to claim. That is why Calvin's particular formulation is helpful: it puts the stress on obedience, rather than, say belief, as the path to knowledge. That is a significant decision." A contemporary form of knowledge through obedience is the current stress on learning through *praxis*. The best theoretical statement of that for church education is Thomas H. Groome, *Christian Religious Education* (New York: Harper and Row, 1980).

28. It is apparent that these various traditions have, in the redaction process, passed through the filter of Deuteronomic theology which is oriented to obedience. That represents something of a changed nuance. First, critically and historically, the new leadership in the exilic period discerned this as an appropriate and faithful response to the demise. See the claim of James Muilenburg, "Baruch the Scribe," in *Proclamation and Presence*, ed. John I. Durham and J. Roy Porter (London: SCM Press, 1970), pp. 215–38, that it was the scribal teachers who had a way to keep faith toward the future. Second, canonically, we cannot deny that this direction of redaction did take place. That is, the canon now given to us is a canon which shapes faith according to obedience. Even if we do not follow such a critical suggestion as that of Muilenburg, canonically, this tilt is not in doubt.

29. On redaction and the canonical process by which wisdom is related to Torah, see Gerald T. Sheppard, *Wisdom as a Hermeneutical Construct*, BZAW 151 (Berlin: Walter de Gruyter, 1980).

30. Samuel Terrien, *Job: Poet of Existence* (Indianapolis: Bobbs Merrill Co., 1957), pp. 171–73.

31. Ibid., p. 170.

32. Terrien, *Elusive Presence*, has explored the ways in which the ethical and aesthetic are in tension in the faith of the Old Testament.

33. R. B. Y. Scott, *Proverbs, Ecclesiastes*, Anchor Bible 18 (Garden City, N.Y.: Doubleday, 1965), p. 256, is characteristic: ". . . provided a safe and simple rule for evidence of intellectual and moral difficulties—Reverence God and observe the laws."

34. See Sheppard, *Wisdom as Hermeneutical*, pp. 121–29. Sheppard argues that vv. 13–14 go well beyond Proverbs and indeed are not precisely

congenial to Proverbs. He argues (against a connection to Proverbs) that these verses have thematic coherence with Qoheleth well beyond Proverbs, and they have most in common with the later traditions of Ben Sirach and Baruch. They are, on this reading, a late, sophisticated articulation of wisdom as an embodiment of Torah. They are, then, not at all a return to what is conventional and safe.

35. Such a positive "moral settlement" of life need not be viewed so critically if James G. Williams is right in "What Does it Profit a Man?: The Wisdom of Qoheleth," *Judaism* 20 (1971): 179–93, reprinted in *Studies in Ancient Israelite Wisdom*, ed. James Crenshaw (New York: KTAV, 1976), pp. 375–89. Williams characterizes Qoheleth as experiencing "a loosing of his self from the world" (p. 386). In that context, clinging to "fear of God" and obedience to Torah is a bold affirmative act at the end.

36. But in its present form, the Torah does not end with ultimate self-seriousness. It adds this statement of openness: "The secret things belong to the Lord our God; but the things that are revealed belong to us and to our children forever, that we may do all the words of this law" (Deut. 29:29). That is, the Torah does not disclose everything. Everything but what is disclosed is retained to the inscrutable God. On this text see Gerhard von Rad, *Deuteronomy* (Philadelphia: Westminster Press, 1966), pp. 180–81, and R. A. Carlson, *David the Chosen King* (Stockholm: Almqvist and Wiksell, 1964), pp. 263–67. Von Rad sees this text as a recognition of the limits of all human wisdom. There is more; not everything is given. But enough has been revealed, and what is revealed is distinctive to Israel and treasured by Israel. This verse is important for us both because of its tilt toward wisdom in the Pentateuch, and because it sets Torah obedience in a context of God's impenetrable mystery. This text appears to me to run toward the Gospel teaching in Matt. 11: 25–27; Luke 10:11–12. On this text see M. Jack Suggs, *Wisdom, Christology and Law in Matthew's Gospel* (Cambridge: Harvard University Press, 1970), pp. 83–97.

37. Joseph Blenkinsopp, *Prophecy and Canon* (South Bend, Ind.: University of Notre Dame Press, 1977).

38. On the centrality of this text, see also Robert Wilson, *Prophecy and Society in Ancient Israel* (Philadelphia: Fortress Press, 1980), pp. 157–66. Although Wilson has no direct concern here for canonical process, his comments are not unrelated to Blenkinsopp's argument.

39. Blenkinsopp, *Prophecy and Canon*, pp. 39, 128.

40. Ibid., p. 132.

41. Ibid., p. 109.

42. Ibid., pp. 151–52.

43. Sheppard, *Wisdom as Hermeneutical*, p. 13.

44. Ibid., p. 119. The last sentence of Blenkinsopp's *Prophecy and Canon* (p. 152) shows how his concern in the prophets and Sheppard's concern in wisdom both attest to the process of keeping the canon alive and functional: "It is this conclusion alone, it seems to me, which justifies our retention of the canon; for as Kierkegaard said, it is not worthwhile to remember that past which cannot become present." Both Blenkinsopp and Sheppard have suggested moves made in the shaping of the canon to permit the past to become present.

45. Terrien, *Elusive Presence*, pp. 112, 121, 172, 182, 201, 279, has contrasted a "religion of the ear" with a "religion of the eye," and has concluded the priority of the ear in Israel's faith.

46. See the critical analysis of this text by Georg Braulik, *Die Mittel Deuteronomischer Rhetorik* (Rome: Biblical Institute Press, 1978), pp. 21–27.

Indexes

AUTHORS